A HISTORY OF THE LITERATURE
OF ADAM AND EVE

SOCIETY OF BIBLICAL LITERATURE

EARLY JUDAISM AND ITS LITERATURE

Number 03

A HISTORY OF THE LITERATURE
OF ADAM AND EVE

by
Michael E. Stone

A HISTORY OF THE LITERATURE OF ADAM AND EVE

by
Michael E. Stone

Scholars Press
Atlanta, Georgia

A HISTORY OF THE LITERATURE OF ADAM AND EVE

by
Michael E. Stone

© 1992
Society of Biblical Literature

Library of Congress Cataloging-in-Publication Data

Stone, Michael E., 1938-
    A history of the literature of Adam and Eve / by Michael E. Stone.
    p. cm. — (Early Judaism and its literature ; no. 03)
    Includes bibliographical references and index.
    ISBN 1-55540-715-3. — ISBN 1-55540-716-1 (pbk.)
    1. Adam (biblical figure) in literature. I. Title. II. Series.
BS580.A4S79 1992
229'.90922—dc20   92-5703
                                                        CIP

Printed in the United States of America
on acid-free paper

This book is dedicated to Marinus de Jonge
Scholar and Friend

Adam & <u>Eve</u>

- Paradise Lost
- references to "mother of all living"?
- Latin version blames Eve?
  - "protoplasts" = Adam & Eve

Books
1) Apocalypse of ~~Adam~~ Moses
2) Life of Adam & Eve

  - "Adam cycle"

TABLE OF CONTENTS

PREFACE

The composition of this book was stimulated by the request I received from Professor M. de Jonge and Professor M.A. Knibb to prepare a lecture on the present state of research on the Books of Adam and Eve for the Seminar on Early Jewish Literature of the SNTS, which devoted its meeting in July 1990 to this topic. That request, of course, did not come out of the blue, and in fact I was actively working at the time on the preparation of a volume of unpublished Armenian Adam texts for eventual publication by the Israel Academy of Sciences and Humanities. Thus, I was glad to be called upon to review the scholarly literature on the Adam books. That review has issued in the present volume.

The literature of Adam and Eve is complex, and it raises a series of difficult technical problems for scholars. These problems can be seen as paradigmatic for a number of aspects of research into the Pseudepigrapha. The difficulties of analyzing the interrelationships of the textual forms, for example, offer a case in which tools developed in the study of other ancient literatures can be applied to pseudepigraphical texts. The complex later history of this literature, particularly in oriental and occidental Christian transmission, highlights issues that scholars of the Pseudepigrapha are coming to realise they cannot avoid. Many of the Pseudepigrapha were transmitted only in Christian contexts. How were they used in those Christian contexts and to what extent were they shaped by them? By what criteria, moreover, are such works identified as Jewish and ancient?

As is explained in the Introductory Remarks, our point of departure has been the primary Adam books, and the question of their origin, date and character. They may have been of Jewish origin and were certainly preserved in Christian tradition, both eastern and western, which fact led us into the questions of the Adam books in medieval Christian literature, and to a lesser extend in medieval Jewish literature. The Islamic Arabic Adam material, as well as the Gnostic and Mandean texts, have been excluded from this study. They contain much of interest, but they are only of tangential interest to this undertaking.

Preface

The purpose of the present book is not to make a new contribution to the resolution of these complex issues. It is to make a clear and integrated assessment and presentation of what is currently known about the various textual, literary and transmission historical aspects of the Adam literature. It is our view that, unless what has been done in the past is properly understood and the methodological implications of past scholarly results are properly conceived, it will be impossible to approach the central issues of meaning, structure, function and message that lie at the heart of what we wish to learn about the Adam books.

The editorial procedure adopted in the present book differs from the normal North American usage in the following way. Since the work is provided with a dense bibliography, it became extremely unwieldy both for the author and the reader to follow the rules governing first citations, short titles, short title lists and the like. Instead, for simplicity's sake, a single bibliographical list was compiled, presented at the end of the book, in strict alphabetical order by author and date. This list contains virtually all the works cited, more than two hundred and fifty in number. In the body of the text, all writings are cited by author and date only, following normal author-date format. This procedure led to simplicity, economy and efficiency of citation.

Although the bibliography cited here is extensive, about fifty works were consulted which were not deemed relevant to the present study. In addition, some thirty works, chiefly articles dealing with medieval literature, were not available to me in the libraries to which I had access. None of the latter seems to me to bear crucially on the subject of the research, and, as far as I can tell, all the writings significant for it have been considered.

I would like to express my thanks for those people who aided me, particularly in retrieving the bibliographical material from the libraries: Valerie Carr, Mark Goodwin and Nicole Sotto. William Adler, Willem Gerritsen, Marinus de Jonge and David Satran were kind enough to read the manuscript and made important comments on it. Gary Anderson and I have worked a good deal together on the Adam literature and he has encouraged me in the present undertaking.

Michael E. Stone
Jerusalem   Tevet 5752 — December 1991

INTRODUCTORY REMARKS

It is a striking fact which we shall not address here that, apart from the beginning of Genesis, Adam and Eve play almost no role in the scriptures of the Hebrew Bible, and certainly the legendary aspects of their doings are not developed in any way in its writings. From the period of the Second Temple on, however, the figures of Adam and Eve, the protoplasts, have always fascinated the nations and cultures whose primordial history is that of Genesis.

Whether it be in painting, in music or in literature, the story of the creation, the transgression and the punishment of the first created ones and their life, children and death, have enthralled people's imagination.[1] What was the Garden really like? What did they eat? How did they sin? What was the first illness they underwent? How did they react to it?

Adam was created in the image of God! (Gen 1:26, 28, 5:1) What a powerful assertion; and that image of God transgressed the divine command. In some lines of thought the theological issues of evil, of sin, of dualism, and a slew of others flowed from this assertion. In generations much prepossessed with issues of sin and evil and the correlative

---

[1]   Rich data on the traditions of Adam and Eve in literature may be found in Evans, 1968, and in Quinn, 1962. Further germane comments may also be found in Murdoch, 1976, 11-13. There are, of course, other studies of this topic, too numerous to mention. Similarly, a number of monographs on the stories of Adam and Eve in art exist and, moreover, the chief features of the iconography of their representation are to be found listed in standard reference works on the subject. Much information on the iconography of the Genesis stories is to be found in M. Alexandre, 1988, *passim* and especially 236. Note the early catacomb discovered on the Via Latina with a painting of Adam and Eve, of much-debated significance: Korol, 1979, 175-190, plates 7-9. Another representation claimed to be of the second to fourth centuries is the amulet published by Goodenough, 1958, while a third one, claimed to be fourth century, was discussed by Troje, 1916.

issues of theodicy and providence, the story of the protoplasts was paradigmatic ("Each man is Adam to his own soul" – *2 Apocalypse of Baruch* 54:19) or constitutive of the present state of affairs.[2]

In addition, for the Christian tradition in particular, the story of the fall of the protoplasts became linked with the economy of redemption; the sin of the first Adam brought death, the death of the last Adam will bring life (1 Cor 15:45-47). So the pattern developed in a wonderful typological intricacy; the Cross stands on Golgotha – on Adam's skull. Christ in his descent to Limbo will break the doors of Hades and free Adam.[3]

Surprisingly, the study of the oldest apocryphal Adam books has been sadly neglected. Considering this neglect on the one hand and the importance of the Adam traditions on the other, a re-assessment of the present state of scholarship on the Adam books is definitely a *desideratum*.[4]

---

[2]   This is implied, of course, by all views claiming that original sin or the state of the world originate from Adam's fall. A survey of scholarly literature concerning Jewish ideas about Adam during the period of the Second Temple may be found in Levison, 1988.

[3]   One of the most striking early sources of this idea is the *Acts of Pilate* (*Gospel of Nicodemus*) which also incorporates many Adam traditions. Some basic approaches of the ancient church to the Adam material are set forth by Simon, 1970, 62-71. Simon points out that early Christian thought treated Adam in a variety of ways, including not just as sinner, but also as tied to Christ by "ce lien organique de continuité qui unit l'embryon à l'homme adulte" or even as a figure exalted above the biblical figures who were considered precursors of Christ (p. 63). On the complex typologies, see, for example, Simon, 1970, 67-69. A similar point is made by Vogl, 1979, 183-185. Vogl's posthumous article does not take cognizance of Simon's remarks. Alexandre, 1988, since she is presenting much of the patristic commentary, contains a great deal of information on these typological exegeses. See especially pp. 293-294 on typologies arising from the Adam story. One medieval exposition of such typology may be discerned in the *Jeu d'Adam*, on which see Vaughan, 1983, 92-93.

[4]   There are narratives about Adam, including a revolt of Iblis, in the Qur'an which are probably dependent on Jewish and Christian apocryphal Adam traditions: see suras 2, 7, 18, and 20. They are not treated in the present work nor are the Adam traditions of Gnosticism or Mandean thought, even

The Range of Books and the Present Work

In the second volume of Charles' *Apocrypha and Pseudepigrapha of the Old Testament*, Wells presented three versions of a life of Adam, one in Greek, one in Latin and one in Old Church Slavonic, this latter, however, only for the beginning of the book.[5] These three versions of the writing about the life of Adam and Eve are clearly related to one another, so that Wells was able to present a synoptic edition of them. An examination of this synopsis quickly reveals that, although there is quite a lot of text that is peculiar to each of the three versions, they also share a very substantial amount of material. Since Wells' time, two further full "primary" Adam books have been discovered and published, one in Armenian and the other in Georgian. The two new "primary" books are closely related; they are designated the Armenian *Penitence of Adam* and the Georgian *Book of Adam*. In addition, the existence of a fragmentary Coptic version has been noted.[6] Consequently, a present-day Wells[7] would have to produce a five- (or even six) column synopsis.[8]

We refer to these versions of the life of Adam as "primary Adam books." This term designates works which appertain to the life of Adam as reflected by the versions just mentioned and which were translated into those versions from Greek (or which survive themselves in Greek). This corpus of primary Adam writings is discussed in the first chapter of the present work.

---

though in the latter instances *books* and not just traditions of Adam are to be observed. See further our remarks in the Preface to the present book.

5   Wells, 1913, 2:123-54.

6   See Chapter 2, section 6, below.

7   The Coptic being so fragmentary, for convenience we shall refer in what follows to the five primary Adam writings which we have in full, without entering a disclaimer about the Coptic on each occasion.

8   Indeed, a synopsis is currently being prepared by the writer in cooperation with G.A. Anderson and W. Lechner-Schmidt. It will include the Greek and Latin texts in the original languages, and translations of the Armenian, Georgian and Slavonic versions.

It is the issue of whether the primary Adam books are Jewish or not that exercises many scholars; that issue is connected with the correlative question of the antiquity of the literature. Is this a corpus of Jewish writings stemming from the period of the Second Temple, which can serve to provide some background to New Testament pronouncements on Adam and his sin? The issues of the date, original language, Jewish character of, and literary relationships between the primary Adam books will be dealt with in the second chapter of this book. As a contribution to the clarification of these issues, a new assessment of all the evidence adduced by scholars for the existence of a Hebrew original of the primary Adam books is included in a special Excursus in this chapter. This new assessment was carried out by Gideon Bohak and the author.

We have assembled the ancient references to the Adam literature, usually designated "Testimonia", in a third chapter which serves to introduce the extensive range of later Jewish and Christian works associated with the protoplasts. It is not always possible to identify the works designated by the testimonia with complete certainty, but the loss of a number of Adam writings in antiquity seems indubitable. The testimonia then, are the only surviving evidence of their existence.

The story of the protoplasts also struck many sympathetic chords in Christian and Gnostic circles; numerous works were written about Adam and Eve and their experiences by Christians and Gnostics. Certain of these writings were very influential in Byzantine and medieval times. They are not Jewish by authorship, nor do they try to appear to be Jewish. In addition, there also exist some medieval Jewish writings of this type. We designate all the later Jewish and Christian writings "secondary Adam books."

The secondary Adam books form a broad literature in a large range of languages. In our treatment of them in Chapter 4 we have attempted to assemble basic information available in published works. Our knowledge and our expertise do not extend to all the languages involved, and we cannot always verify our statements from the sources in the original languages or even aspire to carry out new and independent research on all this literature. Furthermore, particularly in the case of the extensive literature in European vernaculars, our treatment of works written after the first millennium is rather summary and does not claim any measure of completeness.[9] Yet a great deal of interesting material may be found in this literature.

---

9   Given the writer's especial interest in the Armenian Adam books, however, he is able to report on them in greater detail than on works in certain other languages. This is just a reflection of his own capabilities rather than of the value, interest or importance ascribed to any particular literary or linguistic tradition.

CHAPTER 1

THE PRIMARY "JEWISH" ADAM LITERATURE

It is commonly accepted that the oldest form of the apocryphal stories of Adam and Eve is to be found in a group of writings often known collectively as "The Books of Adam and Eve." These writings, the primary Adam books, survive in a variety of languages and in diverse forms. None of them derives from any of the others; they share more or less common material, and each of them is marked by its own peculiarities. Each document has its own difficulties and offers its distinctive challenges. Yet, the distinctiveness of each is best perceived in contrast and comparison with the others. The critical problems engendered by the study of these documents, then, may be formulated at a variety of levels of discussion. If none of the documents is derived from any of the others and they all are translated from Greek, it follows that there existed five (or more) forms of this work in Greek. Thus immediately the issue emerges of the description of the interrelationship between these documents, which is itself largely inseparable from the question of their individual character. The present chapter will deal with the various primary Adam books and present the chief textual and critical problems involved in the investigation of them. In Chapter 2 below, the common and comparative critical issues are discussed.

1. *Apocalypse of Moses*

The Greek book of Adam and Eve is known as *Apocalypse of Moses*. This name was given to it by C. von Tischendorf, presumably because one of the first manuscripts of this work which he discovered is presented as a revelation to Moses. In fact, however, this is a misnomer, since this Mosaic attribution is to be found only in that single manuscript. *Apocalypse of Moses* has been translated into English by Wells,[1] and by M.D. Johnson,[2] as well as into other languages.[3]

---

[1]   Wells, 1913, 2:134-158. On an earlier English translation, see note 6, below.

[2]   Johnson, 1985, 2:249-295.

[3]   The translations into French and German are discussed in notes 6 and 10.

History of the Text

The first edition by von Tischendorf was based on four manuscripts.[4] A second edition was made by Ceriani, independently, two years later, based on a single manuscript.[5] Two further manuscripts were used by the early translators into English and German.[6] Thus by 1900, seven manuscripts were known and five of them had been published. This was far from exhausting the witnesses to the text. A thesis dealing with some aspects of the textual transmission of the *Apocalypse of Moses* was presented in 1969 by J.L. Sharpe.[7] He collated ten new manuscripts, and knew of another seven. Sharpe (and in his footsteps Johnson who translated the work in *OTP*) is not prepared to set any priorities on the manuscripts or groups of manuscripts. As a result, Johnson's translation in *OTP* "takes into account the major variants of all manuscripts." Thus, although Johnson assembled a good deal of new manuscript evidence, his work is not conclusive and his approach lacks clarity and decisiveness as far as the assessment of the variant readings of the different manuscripts is concerned.

The investigation of the Greek text was greatly advanced in a doctoral thesis written for the University of Strasbourg by M. Nagel and presented in 1974.[8] Nagel carried out an exemplary study of the Greek manuscripts, paying careful attention to codicological and contextual aspects of the transmission of the work, as well as to the characteristics of the text itself. He prepared a painstaking variorum edition of the

---

[4] Von Tischendorf, 1866, x-xii, 1-23; his manuscripts are discussed below.

[5] Ceriani, 1868, 19-24.

[6] Fuchs, 1900, 2:506-528; Wells, 1913, 2:123-54. An earlier translation into English was by Walker, 1986 (1870). A second German translation was made by Riessler, 1928, 138-155, with comments on pp. 1273-1274. A Spanish translation was published by Fernandez Marcos, 1983, 325-337.

[7] Sharpe, 1969 [*non vidi*]. His unpublished work was used by M.D. Johnson in his translation in Charlesworth, 1985. Unfortunately, Johnson does not give full details about the manuscripts, so it is difficult fully to reconcile the situation outlined by Sharpe with that in the work of Nagel, about which more below.

[8] Nagel, 1974. His work also contains a concordance of the Greek text of *Apocalypse of Moses*.

Greek manuscripts, presenting the text of each manuscript on a separate line aligned by the words they share. By spacing, he allowed for additions and omissions of individual manuscripts or groups of manuscripts.

However, Nagel did not succeed in producing the full critical edition that his substantial *opus praeparativum* promised. Still, before his premature death, he sent a Greek text to Fr. A.-M. Denis, for use in preparing a concordance of the Greek pseudepigrapha, and this text, which Denis printed, should now be regarded as embodying Nagel's last word on the Greek text.[9]

This problematic textual situation was recently approached by D. Bertrand[10] who attempted to fill the gap left by Nagel's death with an *editio minor* of the Greek text.[11] In his introduction, Bertrand has a most important discussion of the textual tradition of the Greek *Apocalypse of Moses*.[12] However, the text-critical methodology used by Bertrand in the preparation of his edition has been criticized by some reviewers[13] although others are less critical.[14] Thus, today, we still remain without a definitive edition of the Greek text of *Apocalypse of Moses*.

The Manuscripts and Sigla

Von Tischendorf had assigned sigla to his manuscripts, and his system was followed until Sharpe produced his work. Sharp set up a different set of sigla to take account of the additional manuscripts he had discovered. Nagel established yet a third system of sigla which was rather complex, but which encompassed all the manuscripts known to him. His system was simplified by Bertrand, whose edition is in all other respects

---

9   Denis, 1987, ix. Denis prints this text on pp. 813-818 and has concordanced it in his work. This understanding of the intent of Nagel's text was confirmed by Fr. Denis in a conversation in July 1990.

10   Bertrand, 1987a, 37-47. He also translated the book into French with brief notes in Bertrand, 1987b.

11   Bertrand, 1987a.

12   Bertrand, 1987a, 37-47.

13   Stone, 1990.

14   Puech, 1988, 584-585.

dependent on Nagel, as far as the manuscripts and their groupings are concerned. Thus there are now four sets of sigla current. We propose that that of Bertrand be accepted and shall use it ourselves throughout. A table of the Greek manuscripts with their sigla, presented synoptically according to the systems of von Tischendorf, Sharpe, Nagel and Bertrand, is given at the end of this section. Furthermore, the dates of these manuscripts are set forth in the following Table:

Table 1

Manuscripts by Centuries

Century	Siglum	Total
11th century	D	1
13th century	V C	2
13th-14th century	S A	2
14th century	H	1
15th century	P B T R I Z S	7
16th century	K L (1518) M N Q X	6
16th-17th century	F	1
17th century	G	1

It will readily be observed that the largest part of the witnesses were copied in the fifteenth and sixteenth centuries and that the oldest witness is of the eleventh century. It seems likely that the vast majority of surviving Greek copies of the work are now known.[15] Of these manuscripts, Bertrand did not use J, U, W, and Y in his edition. J is a direct copy of I while W was not available for part of the work, and for the rest is almost identical with E.[16]

---

[15]   Denis, 1970, 4, also notes Jassy gr. 49 of the tenth century. This seems to be the oldest known manuscript, but Bertrand observes that it has disappeared (Bertrand, 1987a, 47). He also notes Paris Greek 395, 126v-131v, 16th century. Père Denis was gracious enough to make available to me the as yet unpublished manuscript of the new edition of his work. In this, he gives further details of the Greek manuscripts. We will refer to this as Denis, *Introduction (2nd ed. unpublished)*.

[16]   Bertrand, 1987a, 46. He did not have Y and U at his disposal, nor another manuscript, without siglum: Athens, Bibl. Alexios Kolybas 164, apparently of the 15th century. These sigla are explained in the following Table.

Chapter 1

Table 2

Manuscripts of the *Apocalypse of Moses* and their Sigla

Manuscript	Bert-rand	Tisch-endorf	Sharpe	Nagel
Venice, Bib. Marc. gr. II 42	A	A	A1	A
Vienna, Natbibl. th. gr. 247	B	B		B
Vienna, Natbibl. hist. gr. 67	C	C	C	C
Milan, Bibl. Ambr. C237 inf	D	D	D1	D
Paris, BN gr 1313	E	E1	E1	E1
Montpellier, Med. Sch. H405	F	E2	E2	E2
Andros, Hagias 13	G		D5	AH
Jerusalem, Mar Saba 418	H			J1
Jerusalem, Holy Cross 69	I			J2
Jerusalem, Holy Cross 58	J			J3
Ankara, Soc. hist. tur. 60	K		M1	An
Athens, Nat. Bib. 286	L		D3	At
Patmos, St. John 447	M		H	P1
Patmos, St. John 672	N		M2	P2
Paris, BN grec 395	P			Pa
Brescia, Bib. Quer. A III 3	Q		G	Br
Vatican, Bib. apos. gr. 1192	R		F	Va
Strasbourg, BNU 1913	S		D2	St
Athos, Costamoni 14	T		A2	AC
Sinai, St. Cath. gr. 1936	U			S2
Athos, Vatopedi 422	V		D4	AV
Sinai, St. Cath. gr. 1937	W			S3
Athos, Dochiariou 114	X			AD
Istanbul, St. Sepul. 586	Y			Is
Sinai, St. Cath. gr. 530	Z			S1

Manuscript Groupings

Both Nagel and Sharpe have proposed family groupings of these Greek manuscripts. Their proposals, as reported in the works of Bertrand and Johnson respectively, are most easily to be seen in tabular form.

Table 3

Manuscript Groupings

Nagel	
Family I	D S V K (14:3-43:5) P G B A T L C
Family II	R M
Family III	*N* I *K* (Title-17:2) Q Z H E X F U W

Sharpe[17]	
A	A T
D	D S L V *K N*
C	E F Q
F	R M
	B cannot be classified.

The comparison of these proposed groupings shows that both analyses agree on the group R M; they appear to differ, however, quite substantially regarding the two or three other groups of manuscripts. Even then, on further analysis, the groupings of manuscripts are seen not to conflict, except in the case of K N which Nagel set in Family III with I Q Z H E X F, while Sharpe put them in the same group as D S L V. It is, of course, impossible to judge these issues clearly until a careful study has been made of the stemmatic arguments. Consequently one of the *desiderata* for the study of *Apocalypse of Moses* is a re-examination of the issues of stemmatics and textual groupings. This is a necessary preliminary to the preparation of an *editio minor* or an *editio major* of the text. The criticisms raised about Bertrand's textual methodology make it unlikely that his edition will be serviceable in the long term (see n. 12 above). Nonetheless, there is a great deal of valuable information in his introduction and apparatus, which constitute an advance on the older works by von Tischendorf and of Ceriani.

---

17   So according to Johnson, 1985, 250. We have translated his sigla into those of Bertrand for ease of reference.

Secondary Translation

Johnson refers to "the Armenian" and "the Slavonic" as secondary translations of the Greek text of *Apocalypse of Moses*. By "the Armenian," he apparently means the Armenian *Book of Adam*. This is, indeed, a translation of *Apocalypse of Moses*, and as far as we know, it is the only translation of *Apocalypse of Moses* from Greek into an ancient language. The Slavonic *Vita Adam et Evae*, discussed below in section 3, is not a version of *Apocalypse of Moses*, but is an independent primary Adam book. The Armenian *Book of Adam* was edited by Yovsēp'ianc' from three manuscripts, and many more copies exist.[18] Yovsēp'ianc's manuscripts are:

A   Venice, Mechitarist Old No. 729, *notrgir* undated (perhaps 16th-17th century).
B   Venice, Mechitarist Old No. 633, before 1539.
C   Erevan, Matenadaran, no. 1475 (olim 1631, of the year 1539 C.E.).[19]

In his edition, Yovsēp'ianc' reports that Ms C was copied by F.C. Conybeare in Ejmiacin.[20] Anasyan lists the following further copies in the Matenadaran: nos. 706, 4618, 1978, 4196 and 6686.[21] There are numerous additional copies now listed in manuscript catalogues, and this Armenian text should be re-edited on a broader manuscript base

---

[18]   Yovsēp'ianc', 1898, 1-26. An assessment of this edition, based on a study of the translations of it, is given by Nagel, 1974, 1.239:
> Ce bref contrôle nous a fait entrevoir que l'édition de Venise s'applique à établir un "texte critique" de la *Vie arménienne* sans s'embarrasser des leçons propres à chaque témoin. Le témoin *A* paraît servir d'une manière trop exclusive pour établir le texte critique; mais ce choix est regrettable surtout parce qu'il a dispensé de citer les variantes des deux autres témoins.
Naturally, this situation is exacerbated by the wealth of witnesses now known to exist, still unexploited.

[19]   Anasyan, 1959, 1.238.

[20]   This is also reported by Conybeare, 1894-95, 216-235. He made an English translation of the Armenian text in that article. He notes that some parts of his manuscript were printed by Marr, 1890-91, 228 (*non vidi*).

[21]   Anasyan, 1959, 1.238.

than has been used hitherto. Two English translations of the Armenian *Book of Adam* have been published. One, made by Conybeare, was based on the single Ejmiadzin manuscript, while J. Issaverdens translated Yovsēp'ianc"s text.[22] A German translation was made by E. Preuschen.[23]

Conybeare was of the opinion that this Armenian text "seems to have been made not from a Greek, but from a Syriac or Ethiopic, or even Arabic text,"[24] but this was denied and his arguments were controverted by Preuschen who energetically maintained that the original was Greek.[25] Preuschen's view in this matter seems to be correct. Nagel regards the Armenian *Book of Adam* as a witness to his third recension of the *Apocalypse of Moses*, together with Greek manuscripts N I J K.[26] The Armenian version was dated by Conybeare probably to the fifth or sixth century, but in any case prior to 1000.[27]

Literary Issues

Various analyses of the structure and contents of the Greek *Apocalypse of Moses* have been made, recently by Bertrand and Levison. In general terms Bertrand maintains the distinction between two parts of *Apocalypse of Moses*: a story based on the first chapters of Genesis and a story of the burial of the protoplasts. He further discerns subdivisions within these parts, but strongly upholds the unity of the work.[28] In addition to his analysis of the contents, he gives a list of the

---

22   Conybeare, 1894-95; Issaverdens, 1901, 21-42.

23   Preuschen, 1900, 163-252, and *separatim*. We have consulted this work in the *separatim* form. The translation of the Armenian *Book of Adam* is to be found there on pp. 7-24.

24   Conybeare, 1894-95, 216. Compare also, Fuchs, 1900, 506.

25   Preuschen, 1900, 4-6.

26   Nagel, 1974, 1.212-254.

27   Denis, 1970, 5, n. 12 and sources cited there. Denis confounds the Armenian version of *Apocalypse of Moses* with the other Armenian Adam works. The question of the dating, of course, requires reassessment.

28   Bertrand, 1987a, 50-54, where he gives a detailed analysis of the book.

major aspects of biblical exegesis in it,[29] and deals in some detail also
with the chief ideas expressed by the text.[30]

Context

Levison regards *Apocalypse of Moses* as divided into four sections: an Introduction (1:1-5:1); The Quest for the Oil of Life (5-13); The
Testament of Eve (14-30); and The Pardoning and Burial of Adam (31-
43). He characterizes each of the sections at some length.[31] He claims
that the dominant purpose of *Apocalypse of Moses* is to present Adam
"as a forgiven sinner who endures the pain of existence, faces death with
uncertainty, but receives mercy after death."[32] He notes the important
parallel between Seth's quest for the oil and Adam's quest for fruit of
the tree of life (chaps. 27-29).[33]

Parts of the story of the Latin *Vita Adam et Evae* do not occur
in *Apocalypse of Moses*. Thus the story of the repentance (Latin *Vita
Adam et Evae* 1-17) is not found in the vast majority of manuscripts of
Apocalypse of Moses, although it occurs in two manuscripts (R and M).
Chapters 15-30 form a narrative that is not found in the Latin *Vita Adam
et Evae* and which has been called a 'Testament of Eve.'[34] This is discussed further below, in Chapter 2 where the interconnections of the
various Adam books are presented,[35] and other literary issues are discussed.

2. Latin *Vita Adam et Evae*

The Latin version of the primary Adam book is commonly known by
the name *Vita Adam et Evae*. Sparks notes that the occurrence in it of

---

[29]   Bertrand, 1987a, 54-56.

[30]   Bertrand, 1987a, 57-60.

[31]   Levison, 1988, 164-173.

[32]   Levison, 1988, 164.

[33]   Levison, 1988, 170.

[34]   Denis, 1970, 3.

[35]   Some general remarks may be found in Charlesworth, 1981, 159-160. He
        also comments on the *Cave of Treasures* on pp. 91-92 and the Latin *Vita
        Adam et Evae* on pp. 74-75.

transliterated Greek words makes it certain that it is a translation of a Greek original.[36]

There have been three main studies of the textual history of the document. The first was by W. Meyer, who published a critical text based almost solely on the Latin manuscripts in Munich. Next, J.H. Mozley published another list of manuscripts and a Latin text, concentrating exclusively on those manuscript copies found in Britain. Third, most recently, M.E.B. Halford published an extensive list of manuscripts drawn from a wide range of provenances.[37] The Latin *Vita Adam et Evae* was translated into English by Wells in Charles' *APOT* together with the Greek *Apocalypse of Moses* and parts of the Slavonic *Life of Adam*, and by M.D. Johnson in Charlesworth's *OTP* together with the Greek *Apocalypse of Moses*. In *The Apocryphal Old Testament,* M. Whittaker chose to translate only the Latin *Vita Adam et Evae*, giving the Greek *Apocalypse of Moses* 25-30 in an Appendix.[38] The Latin *Vita Adam et Evae* has also been translated into other modern languages.

Manuscripts and Editions

The text was best edited over 100 years ago by Meyer on the basis of twelve manuscripts (nearly all in Munich) and a number of medieval European versions.[39] Additional textual information was published by Mozley, who added a number of British manuscripts to those used by

---

[36]   Sparks, 1984, 143. In that volume, the introductory remarks on the Adam literature were written by Sparks. German translations of the Latin *Vita Adam et Evae* were prepared by Fuchs, 1900 and by Riessler, 1928, 668-681, with comments on pp. 1311-1312. An Italian translation was made from Meyer's text by Piatelli, 1968-69, 9-23. The work was translated into Spanish by Fernandez Marcos, 1983, 338-352.

[37]   References to all these works may be found in the following paragraphs where they will be discussed in detail. A brief summary of the situation of the Latin text was included by Brian O. Murdoch in his article: Murdoch, 1973a, 209-223; see particularly pp. 211-213.

[38]   Whittaker, 1984, 141-167. In fact, this selection of material provides a fairly inclusive representation of the contents of the work.

[39]   Meyer, 1878, 187-250. He discusses the manuscripts and translations of the *Vita Adam et Evae* on pp. 209-220 of his publication. The information given below is drawn from his work, supplemented by that in Mozley's, Denis' and Halford's writings.

Meyer. Another Latin text was printed by Eis in 1935, based on two manuscripts, Admont 25 and Zwettl 13.[40] Further lists of manuscripts were made by Stegmüller[41] and recently, most exhaustively by Halford.[42]

Meyer identified four manuscript groups, and Mozley added further information about certain of these, and also identified a fifth group. A further subgroup of Meyer's Group III was identified by Thomson.[43]

Meyer's Group I

S	Codex Clm 17740 (St. Mang. 10) s. ix, fol. 37.
T	Codex Clm. 18525^b (Tegerns. 525^b) s. x, fol. 90.
M	Codex Clm. 19112 (Tegerns. 1112) s. xii, fol. 156.

Mss S T and M are closely related. Additional copies of this group are to be found in four fifteenth-century manuscripts, all in Munich: nos. 5604, fol. 156; 7685, fol. 122; 11740, fol. 291 and 11796, fol. 152. Meyer did not use these later copies of Group I.

Meyer's Group II

(17)	Codex Clm. 17151, parchment, s. xiii-xiv, fol. 27.
(5)	Codex Clm. 5865, s. xv, fol. 342.
(9)	Codex Clm. 9022, s. xv, fol. 311.
(3)	Codex Cgm. 3866, s. xv, fol. 195.

Meyer is of the opinion that this recension existed about 730 C.E. (see below, on Group IV). It has a long expansion following Chapter 29 and another at the end, which latter relates how Solomon found and read tablets set up by Seth. The medieval translations and reworkings in European tradition which were known to Meyer nearly all go back to this recension. Such translations exist in French, in English (including a

---

[40]   Eis, 1967, 241-255.

[41]   Stegmüller, 1950 gives many details of manuscripts: nos. 74-74.10, pp. 26-27. He lists nine further copies.

[42]   Halford, 1981, 417-427: W. Lechner-Schmidt informs me privately of the existence of yet further Latin manuscripts.

[43]   Thomson, 1933, 271-278. Halford's views regarding groups of manuscripts are of a different character and are considered below.

number of verse renderings), Italian and German.[44] Mozley identified three groups of manuscripts which are affiliated with Meyer's Group II. The following two manuscripts are related most closely to it and he designates them "(ii):"

D	Harleian 495, s. xiv.
Q	Queen's Oxford 213, s.xv.

His eight Group "(i)" manuscripts are also related to Meyer's Group II, but include special passages at the end, dealing with the formation of Adam's body and the giving of his name.[45] Mozley says that "it is almost certain that all these MSS are derived from one original."[46] The following are the members of this group:

A	Arundel 326, s. xiv.
R	Royal 8 F xvi, s. xiv.
C	Harleian 526, s. xiv.
L	Lambeth 352, s. xiv.
E	Harleian 275, s. xv.
F	Harleian 2432, s. xv.
J	St. John's Cambridge 176, s. xv.
P	Corpus Christi Cambridge 275, s. xv.

---

[44]   See Meyer, 1878, 210-214. Further medieval renderings exist, which have come to light since Meyer's day: see Chapter 4 below, particularly sections 9 and 11. The relationship between these medieval renderings and the Latin text should be further investigated. Below, the influence of the Latin *Vita Adam et Evae* on northwest Slavonic literature is pointed out. Furthermore, a translation of the Latin into Croatian also exists: see below, note 56.

[45]   Then he compares this with the material published by Förster, 1907-1908, 477-529. This is part of a complex literary tradition: see below, chapter 4, section 2.

[46]   Mozley, 1929, 121. He also mentions two incunabula in the British Museum, identical with one of those used by Katona, *Magyar Tudomanos Akad*. köt. 18, sz. 10 (1904), (*non vidi*), and witnessing to Meyer's Group III (*ibid*). A.C. Dunstan studied the points at which Lutwin's *Adam und Eva* differs from Latin *Vita Adam et Evae* as published by Meyer. He argued that these points often reflect different Latin readings unknown to Meyer. He examined eleven manuscripts of the Latin *Vita Adam et Evae* from Britain that were subsequently published by Mozley and analyzed a number of passages in this vein: see Dunstan, 1929, 191-99.

Finally, as his group "(iii)" Mozley identified a much abbreviated version of his group "(ii)," which is also, naturally, related to Meyer's Group II. This occurs in one manuscript, viz.:

>   *W*   Winchester Cathedral, early s. xiii.

Meyer's Group III

>   *(4)*   Codex Clm. 4656, s. xv, fol. 214.
>   *(15)*   Codex Clm. 15610, s. xv, fol. 165.
>   *(18)*   Codex Clm. 18406, s. xv, fol. 95.
>   *(2)*   Codex Clm. 2778, s. xv, fol. 264.

This text has minor additions and omissions at various places. Moreover, it omits Chapter 51 a-d, but tells the story of the wood of the Cross in four large additions in Chapters 42-44, 48.[47] Some discussions of this textual tradition have been written.[48] A separate subgroup of this text type was identified by Thomson.[49] It may be found in the five incunabula editions of the Latin *Vita Adam et Evae* and in one manuscript, Huntington Library HM 1342 of the fifteenth century. The most striking aspect of this subgroup is an additional two chapters at the beginning, based largely on Gen 3.[50]

Meyer's Group IV

>   P   Paris, BN latin 5327.

This text has certain of the additions mentioned above, but is also much abbreviated. Codicological considerations lead to the conclusion that this manuscript was made from an original dating between 730 and 740, making it an exceptionally old witness to the text.

---

[47] Some further witnesses and forms of this textual type are mentioned by Meyer, 1878, 215 including an incunabulum, a French translation, and a German poem.

[48] Halford, 1981. Eis, 1935, 64 notes, following in Meyer's footsteps, the particular relationship of the Middle High German poem *Adam und Eva* by Lutwin with Group III type manuscripts. However, this is the object of some discussion: see Eis, 1935, 66-72.

[49] Thomson, 1933.

[50] Thomson, 1933, 275-278 published this material and also some comparisons with other group of manuscripts.

Mozley's Group "(iv)"

B   Balliol 228, s. vx.

This is a compilation of the *Vita Adam et Evae* with the legend of the Holy Rood, parts of which occurred in Meyer's Group III. They are combined with the material on Adam's body and name to form a connected narrative.[51]

Recently, a study of the Latin textual tradition was carried out by M.E.B. Halford.[52] Halford prepared a list of all known manuscripts, consulting the published editions and catalogues of manuscripts. She listed a total of seventy-three manuscripts, and it is possible that even more exist.[53] Her list also indicates the affiliations of some of these manuscripts and provides brief bibliography for them. A much abbreviated form of her list is given at the end of this section.

The Text and Its Problems

Meyer's text is fundamentally based on Group I of manuscripts, but he often has recourse to readings of Groups II and III. The fact that Meyer selected Group I as his text[54] has influenced scholarship of the Latin *Vita Adam et Evae*, since it is Meyer's text that scholars usually investigate, not his apparatus. Mozley's text is based on the Arundel manuscript which gives the document a different cast.

Some most interesting comments on the evaluation of the manuscripts were made by Halford. She commences by pointing out that, although Meyer refers to his Group I as the earliest form of the text, in fact it is the text preserved in the oldest Munich manuscripts, and that Meyer's criterion for selecting it as a base was that it provided "einen festen und lesbaren Text."[55] Furthermore, considering the complexity of the manuscript traditions, Halford comments: "Rather than

---

51   Mozley, 1929, 122. The literature on the Holy Rood legend is discussed
       by Murdoch, 1973a, 213.

52   Halford, 1981, 417-427.

53   Halford, 1981, 421-427.

54   Meyer, 1878, 219; see also Halford, 1981, 418.

55   See Halford, 1981, 418-19 for a full discussion of this issue.

classes with interpolations it is perhaps safer to speak of a group of elements or narrative units, many of which are found together regularly in set patterns. ... Each MS can be seen as containing the sum of what was known about Adam and Eve at a particular time and place".[56] In light of this approach she queries whether it is possible to establish a proper critical edition of this text, but considers it extremely important to gain insight into whether Meyer's and Mozley's division of the manuscripts is accurate.

This problem is thrown into high relief, moreover, when we consider the fact that much additional material occurs in the other groups of manuscripts. Should these additional passages be seen as mere secondary expansions? Some of them were exceedingly important in the medieval European development of the Adam traditions. The chief extensive additions have been categorized by Murdoch. According to Group III, on Cain's birth, Eve wants to kill him. In the context of a vision, Groups II and IV insert a prophecy of the future in Adam's narrative to Seth about the fall. In the Group III manuscripts a Holy Rood tale follows the end of the book. Seth places seeds or twigs from Paradise into the dead Adam's mouth which become the tree of the Cross. In Group II, Seth's stelae are discovered by Solomon.[57]

Mozley discusses the character of the additional passages found in his manuscripts in some detail. In particular he stresses manuscripts containing additional Sethite and Holy Rood portions and the account of the formation and naming of Adam.[58] He observes that certain of

---

[56] Halford, 1981, 419. She sees the vernacular versions as further points along this continuum. It is perhaps appropriate to remark that Jagič, in Chapter 7 of his study of the Slavonic *Vita Adam et Evae,* referred to in the next section, discussed the influence of the Latin *Vita Adam et Evae* on northwest Slavonic literature, in Bohemian and Polish (pp. 64-69). Turdeanu, 1981, 437 observes that the Croatian version of the primary Adam book was made from the Latin.

[57] Halford, 1981, 18-19.

[58] See also Murdoch, 1976, 19-20. The account of the creation of Adam is dealt with below, in Chapter 4, under the title *Adam Octipartite.* The account of the naming, in particular, belongs with the versions of Latin *Vita Adam et Evae:* see Murdoch, *ibid,* 20.

these echo material to be found in Slavonic *Vita Adam et Evae*.[59] We might add that a comparison with the Armenian *Penitence of Adam* and the Georgian *Book of Adam* is also likely to show certain common points.[60] Halford confirms Mozley's comments about the additional passages which she shows to exist on their own as well as in various of the manuscript groups. Her approach is reflected in the quotation given above, in which she queries the assumptions underlying the stemmatic work of Meyer in particular.[61]

Halford also draws attention to the vernacular versions of the Latin *Vita Adam et Evae*. Meyer had already known of some versions in French, English, Italian and German. Referring to the work of Greene, Kelley and Murdoch on the *Saltair na Rann*, she mentions additional texts in German, Breton, and Italian.[62] A.C. Dunstan, in a study of the Middle English poem *Canticum de Creatione* shows that nearly all the peculiarities observed in that text when it is compared with Meyer's edition disappear when the broader base of comparison adduced by Mozley is brought into account.[63] Indeed, the relationships of the vernacular versions to the Latin, and to one another, are impossible to deter-

---

[59] Mozley, 1929, 123. He also notes, on p. 125, that the early English text of Adam's life edited in 1885 derives from his Ms L: see further on this in Chapter 4, section 12.

[60] The complexity of the whole tradition is shown by the fact that the incident of the penitence occurs in certain Greek manuscripts, as Nagel already showed. In the *Gospel of Bartholomew*, printed by Vassiliev, 1893, 19-20 is a passage explaining Satan's fall in terms and language strikingly like that of the Latin, Armenian and Georgian forms of chap. 14 of the primary Adam book. Here again, a unit of material, not preserved in the Greek *Apocalypse of Moses*, is reflected in a Greek text. The *Gospel of Bartholomew* in Greek probably goes back to the fifth century. See on this Turdeanu, 1981, 329-31.

[61] See the discussion of these texts below in Chapter 4.

[62] Halford, 1981, 416 refers to Murdoch, 1976, 2.25-31.

[63] Dunstan, 1931, 431-442. He also discussed another Middle English poem to be found in Ms. Auchinl. Edinb. Advoc. Libr. This latter manuscript was the source of one text of the *Canticum de Creatione* published by C. Horstmann, 1878, 139-147. He also published a text from another manuscript, Oxford, Trinity College, 57, *ibid*, 124-138. See further, chapter 3 below on these poems.

mine without a fuller edition of the Latin, giving all the "additional" passages to be found in the various Latin recensions.

In our judgment, Halford's comments are significant, though they are not completely satisfactory (see below). The presently known Latin text must be regarded as largely tentative, until at least sample collations and a preliminary classification of all the known manuscripts are undertaken. The role of the vernacular versions in the knowledge of the text should be clarified. Moreover, some of the material found in manuscripts other than those of Meyer's Group I, which is often considered "secondary" or "interpolated", may come, as both Mozley and Halford observe, from rather ancient sources.[64]

Date

Meyer observed that the Latin *Vita Adam et Evae* was translated later than the Latin of *The Gospel of Nicodemus* and consequently after the third or fourth century C.E.[65] He also adduced arguments to show that the ancestor of his Ms P was written between 730 and 740. The ensuing history of the text was unclear to him, except that it had a most extensive influence in medieval European literature. Mozley thinks he may have found an uncial error in his group "(i)", another indication of the eighth century date *ante quem* of the Latin *Vita Adam et Evae*.[66] On the basis of literary and textual arguments, he would set the ancestor of his manuscripts W, D, Q, and B at the twelfth century at the latest.[67] No

---

[64] This view is echoed by Sparks who opines that there is much additional material in the Latin *Vita Adam et Evae*: some old and Jewish (e.g. chaps. 50-51) and other parts Christian (e.g. 41:2-42:5 taken from *Acts of Pilate*).

[65] According to F. Scheidweiler (*apud* R. Hennecke and W. Schneemelcher, *New Testament Apocrypha*, trans. R.M. Wilson, 447) by the time of Epiphanius in *Haer*. 50.1 (ca. 375 C.E.), "the *Grundschrift* [i.e. of the *Gospel of Nicodemus* M.E.S.] at any rate was in existence, but possibly already in an expanded version as compared with the original." This dating would probably make us push Meyer's date down some decades.

[66] Mozley, 1929, 125.

[67] Mozley, 1929, 127.

new considerations bearing on the date of the Latin *Vita Adam et Evae* have been adduced since Mozley's time.[68]

Issues in Research

Almost none of the discussions we have seen has dealt in any detail with the purpose, shape or function of this version, nor with it in comparison with the Greek *Apocalypse of Moses* or with other primary Adam writings. The only exception, to a limited extent, is the work of Levison in his book *Portraits of Adam*. He proposes that the Latin *Vita Adam et Evae* is divided into two main parts and that each such part contains three subsections. The two main parts are chapters 1-29 and 30-48. In each main part he discerns a quest (1-8 and 30-36 + 40); an interruption by Satan (9-17 and 37-39); and an outcome of the quest (18-29 and 41-48).[69] The chief purpose of Latin *Vita Adam et Evae* he proposes is "to exonerate Adam and denigrate Eve, thus presenting the readers with a perfect penitent, a righteous figure who receives mercy during life and after death."[70] He supports this analysis with a presentation of the contents of the book (pp. 175-183) concluding that three major points dominate this: that God grants mercy for proper penitence; that Satan's enmity persists against the image of God; and that Adam is righteous and Eve to blame for the present plight.[71] As was true of his analysis of *Apocalypse of Moses*, here too Levison does not concern himself with the possible function of the book in its Christian context, nor does he deal in any depth with the interrelationship of the two versions he chose to present. Yet his analysis goes beyond anything existing so far.

One wonders how the relationship of Latin *Vita Adam et Evae* with Greek *Apocalypse of Moses*, or else an assessment of the primary or secondary nature of its special materials, could be carried out without first gaining a better picture of its development and functioning in the

---

68   Murdoch, 1973a, speaks of a fourth century date, although the basis for this is unclear (p. 209).

69   Levison, 1988, 174.

70   Levison, 1988, 164.

71   Levison, 1988, 184.

context of medieval literature. It was Murdoch who devoted some remarks to this, and we quote his apt comments at length:

> The VA [*Vita Adam et Evae*] does not exist, then, in a single
> text, but is rather a labile sequence of distinct chapters. Even at
> its earliest stages there are elements that appear to be contrac-
> tions or expansions of passages attested at greater or lesser
> length in say, AM [Greek *Apocalypse of Moses*]. ... Emphases
> may shift more clearly in the comparison of the extant versions
> with one another. ... The context of the VA must also be con-
> sidered (both with regard to the Latin texts and more especially
> with the vernacular adaptations). ... The work is frequently seen
> as a preface to the Holy Rood material, for example, but it also
> forms part of a chronicle presentation of world history without
> the explicit soteriological bias.[72]

Murdoch's remarks share aspects with those of Halford quoted above.
Murdoch suggests that the configuration of the text is to a considerable
extent determined by context and function. Halford suggests that it is
determined by time and place. In common to both approaches
(between which there is no necessary contradiction) is a strong sense of
the great variety of text types and configurations to be observed in the
different groups of manuscripts of the Latin *Vita Adam et Evae* and in
its various vernacular translations and reworkings.

If this approach is accepted, then, of course, the mode by which
an edition is to be prepared becomes difficult to comprehend, for each
particular crystallization of the text is a thing in itself and issues of priority and posteriority seem to become irrelevant. Yet this cannot be
completely so: some manuscripts were obviously copied from others;
certain reworkings were equally clearly made from one textual type
rather than another. Manuscripts can be dated, sometimes recensions
or reworkings can too. We venture to suggest that, before completely
abandoning more traditional paradigms of textual development, they
be explored thoroughly as far as they can be applied to the Latin *Vita
Adam et Evae* and its vernacular translations. This does not exclude
bringing the factors of time and place, or of function and use to bear in
the textual analysis, but it does imply first using these factors to assess
and understand the textual development of the work. Only with the
exhaustion of the benefits to be derived from them (and there will as-

---

[72]   Murdoch, 1976, 20.

suredly be some) should the traditional paradigms be set aside. Then innovative approaches to understanding textual variety can, and should, be sought and in this search the remarks of Halford and Murdoch will receive redoubled significance.

It might be remarked that not only in the case of the manuscripts and recensions of Latin primary Adam writing are scholars faced by the bewildering polymorphy of the text. The relationship between the primary Adam writings themselves is equally mystifying. These problems will be addressed in the next chapter.

A List of the Latin Manuscripts of Vita Adam et Evae

ABERYSTWYTH.—The National Library of Wales MS 335A (Hengwrt 239); 14th century, fols. 131-40. This probably belongs to Mozley's "Arundel" class.

ADMONT.—Stiftsbibliothek MS 25; 13th century, parchment, fols. 270-72v = Eis A.

BRUSSELS.—Bibliothèque Royale Albert 1er MS IV F.15; mid 15th century, paper, fols. 1-11v.

CAMBRIDGE 1.—Corpus Christi College MS 275; 15th century, parchment, fols. 9-14 = Mozley P; Stegmüller 74, 7.1

CAMBRIDGE 2.—St John's College MS 176; 15th century, parchment, fols. 67-74 = Mozley J; Stegmüller 74, 7.1.

CHICAGO.—Newberry Library MS Ry 6; 11th/12th century, fols. 224r-228v.

COPENHAGEN.—Royal Library, Ny Kgl. Saml. MS 123; 15th century, paper, fols. 47v-49v = Stegmüller 74,3.

DONAUESCHINGEN.—Hofbibliothek MS 449; 15th century, paper, fols. 1-5r.

DUBLIN.—Trinity College MS 509; 15th century, parchment. Related to Mozley D + Q. No siglum in Mozley; Stegmüller 74, 7.1.

GRAZ.—Universitätsbibliothek MS 904 (38/3); 15th century, paper, fols. 164-169v = Class II. Meyer's MS 33/3 (p. 210n.) = Stegmüller 74, 10.

LONDON 1.—British Library MS Arundel 326; 13th/14th century, parchment, fols. 42-50 = Mozley A; Stegmüller 74, 7.1.

LONDON 2.—British Library MS Royal 8 1 XVI; 14th century, parchment, fols. 55-59 = Mozley R; Stegmüller 74, 7.1.

LONDON 3.—British Library MS Harley 495; 14th century, parchment, fols. 43-50 = Mozley D; Stegmüller 74, 7.1. *VA* 1-7 missing.

LONDON 4.—British Library MS Harley 526; 14th century, parchment, fols. 68-77 = Mozley C; Stegmüller 74, 7.1.

LONDON 5.—Lambeth Palace Library MS 352; 14th century, parchment, fols. 1-4 = Mozley L; Stegmüller 74, 7.

LONDON 6.—British Library MS Harley 275; 15th century, paper, fols. 153-158v = Mozley E; Stegmüller 74, 7.1.

LONDON 7.—British Library MS Harley 2432; 15th century, parchment, fols. 1-10 = Mozley F; Stegmüller 74, 7.1.

LONDON 8.—British Library MS Sloane 289; 15th century, parchment, fols. 70v-79v. No siglum given by Mozley who regards it as a close copy of Mozley A; = Stegmüller 74, 7.1. Fols. 70v-73v contain the Holy Rood legend.

LONDON 9.—Inner Temple Library MS Petyt 538 Vol. 36; 15th century, paper, fols. 140-148. Belongs to Mozley's "Arundel" class.

LUND.—Medeltid MS 30; fol. 144-153 = Stegmüller 74, 6.1.

MUNICH 1.—Bayerische Staatsbibliothek clm 17740 (St.Mang. 10); 10th and 11th centuries, parchment, fols. 37-46 = Meyer S (Class I); Stegmüller 74, 10.

MUNICH 2.—Bayerische Staatsbibliothek clm 18525b (Teg. 525b); 10th century, parchment fols. 89-95 = Meyer T (Class I); Stegmüller 74, 10.

MUNICH 3.—Bayerische Staatsbibliothek clm 19112 (Teg. 1111); 12th century, parchment fols. 156-162 = Meyer M (Class I); Stegmüller 74, 10.

MUNICH 4.—Bayerische Staatsbibliothek clm 21534 (Weihenst. 34); 12th century, parchment fol. 101 = Meyer (21) Class II.

MUNICH 5.—Bayerische Staatsbibliothek clm 17151 (Scheftl. 151); 12th century, parchment fol. 177 = Meyer (17) Class II; Stegmüller 74, 6.

MUNICH 6.—Bayerische Staatsbibliothek clm 4350 (Aug.S.Ulr. 50); 14th century, paper, fols. 28-29 = Meyer (43) Class II.

MUNICH 7.—Bayerische Staatsbibliothek clm 2778 (Ald. 248); 15th century, paper, fol. 227. Class III.

MUNICH 8.—Bayerische Staatsbibliothek clm 2778 (Ald. 248); 15th century, paper, fol. 264 = Meyer (2) Class III; Stegmüller 74, 10.

MUNICH 9.—Bayerische Staatsbibliothek clm 2800 (Ald. 270); 15th century, paper, fols. 240-50. Class III.

MUNICH 10.—Bayerische Staatsbibliothek clm 4756 (Bened. 256); 15th century, paper, fols. 192-200 = Meyer (4) Class III; Stegmüller 74, 10.

MUNICH 11.—Bayerische Staatsbibliothek clm 5604 (Diess. 104); 15th century, paper, fols. 156-59. Class I; Stegmüller 74, 10.

MUNICH 12.—Bayerische Staatsbibliothek clm 5865 (Ebersb. 65); 15th century, paper, fols. 342-45 = Meyer (5) Class II; Stegmüller 74, 6.

MUNICH 13.—Bayerische Staatsbibliothek clm 5976 (Ebersb. 176); 15th century, paper, fol. 82. Class III.

MUNICH 14.—Bayerische Staatsbibliothek clm 7685 (Ind. 285); 15th century, paper, fols. 122-26. Class I; Stegmüller 74, 10.

MUNICH 15.—Bayerische Staatsbibliothek clm 9022 (Mon.Frans. 322); 15th century, paper, fols. 311-17 = Meyer (9) Class II; Stegmüller 74, 6.

MUNICH 16. — Bayerische Staatsbibliothek clm 11740 (Polling. 440); 15th century, paper, fols. 291-97. Class I; Stegmüller 74, 10.

MUNICH 17.—Bayerische Staatsbibliothek clm 11796 (Polling. 496); 15th century, paper, fols. 152-55. Class I; Stegmüller 74, 10.

MUNICH 18.—Bayerische Staatsbibliothek clm 15610 (Rot. I 10); 15th century, paper, fols.165-68 = Meyer (15) Class III; Stegmüller 74, 10.

MUNICH 19.—Bayerische Staatsbibliothek clm 18406 (Teg. 406); 15th century, paper, fols. 95-98 = Meyer (18) Class III; Stegmüller 74, 10.

MUNICH 20.—Bayerische Staatsbibliothek clm 26630; 15th century, paper, fols. 351-53.

MUNICH 21.—Bayerische Staatsbibliothek cgm 3866; 15th century, paper, fols. 194-99 = Meyer (3) Class II; Stegmüller 74, 6.

MUNICH 22.—Bayerische Staatsbibliothek clm 11601 (Polling. 301); 14th century, fols. 87-88.

MUNICH 23.—Bayerische Staatsbibliothek clm 16472 (S.Zen. 72); 14th century, fols. 165-73. Cf. Stuttgart MS.

MUNICH 24.—Bayerische Staatsbibliothek clm 17668 (Semansh. 68); 15th century, fols. 77-83.

MUNICH 25.—Bayerische Staatsbibliothek clm 18597 (Teg. 597); 15th century, fol. 273.

MUNICH 26.—Bayerische Staatsbibliothek clm 23929 (ZZ. 929); 15th century, fols. 32-35.

NAMUR.—Bibliothèque du Musée Archéologique MS 162; 15th century, paper, fols. 128r-131r = Stegmüller 74, 6.1

OXFORD 1.—Queens College MS 213; 15th century, parchment, fols. 1-8: VA fols. 14-18. Belongs to Mozley's "Arundel" class.[73]

OXFORD 2.—Balliol College MS 228; 14th/15th century, fols. 203-06v = Mozley B; Stegmüller 74, 7.1

---

[73]   Halford lists this as "Oxford 3," but obviously it should be "Oxford 1"; this is presumably a typographical error.

OXFORD 3.—Queens College Ms 213; 15th century, parchment, fols. 1-8 = Mozley Q; Stegmüller 74, 7.1

PARIS 1.—Bibliothèque Nationale MS lat. 5327; 9th century, parchment, fols. 83-87 = Meyer P (Class IV); Stegmüller 74, 10.

PARIS 2.—Bibliothèque Nationale MS lat. 590; 14th/15th century, parchment and paper, fols. 163-68.

PRAGUE 1.—Universita Karlova Library MS 789 [V.A.7. (Y.111.2. n.7.)]; 14th century, fols. 196r-200r.

PRAGUE 2.—Universita Karlova Library MS 1914 [X.E.13. (Y.111.4. n.48.)]; 14th century, fols. 85v-88v.

PRAGUE 3.—Universita Karlova Library MS 2619 [(XIV.G.II.]; 14th/15th century, fols. 132r—37v.

PRAGUE 4.—Universita Karlova Library MS 2032 [XI.C.8.]; 15th century, fols. 206v-09r.

ROUEN.—Bibliothèque municipale de Rouen MS 1462 (U.65); 14th century, parchment, fol. 245.

SAN MARINO, CA.—H.E. Huntington Library MS HM 1342; 15th century, paper, fols. 4r-14v = Stegmüller 74, 6.2.

SCHLÄGL 1.—Stiftsbibliothek MS 156. Cpl. 818. 145; 15th century, paper, fols. 405v-409v = Stegmüller 74, 2.

SCHLÄGL 2.—Stiftsbibliothek MS 198. Cpl. 820. 126; 15th century, paper, fols. 1-4v.

ST. GALL.—Stiftsbibliothek MS 927; 15th century, paper, fols. 225-35.

STRÄNGNÄS.—Domkyrkbiblioteket Q.16 (Op.1); 15th century, fols. 5r-9r = Stegmüller 74, 2.

STUTTGART.—Würtembergische Landesbibliothek MS HB XII 20; 14th century, paper, fols. 132ra-34vb. Referred by the cataloguers to Munich 23.

VALENCIENNES.—Bibliothèque municipale, MS 168 (160); late 13th century, parchment, fol. 241.

VIENNA 1.—Österreichische Nationalbibliothek Cod. Vindob. 1628
[Rec.2015.a); mid-14th century, fols. 98v-101v. Class III (Meyer, p.
210n.).

VIENNA 2.—Österreichische Nationalbibliothek Cod. Vindob. 1629
[Rec.3129]; mid-14th century, fols. 98v-110v. Class II (Meyer, p.
210n.).

VIENNA 3.—Österreichische Nationalbibliothek Cod. Vindob. 1355
[Lunael.Q.114]; 14/15th century, fols. 92r-97v. Class II (Meyer, p.
210n.).

VIENNA 4.—Österreichische Nationalbibliothek Cod. Vindob.2809
[Rec.3006]3; 15th century, paper, fols. 308v-310v. Class II (Meyer,
p.210n.).

WERTHEIM.—Evangelische Kirchenbibliothek MS 726 = Stegmüller 74, 5.

WINCHESTER.—Cathedral Library MS VII; 13th century, parchment, fols.
109v-112r = Mozley W.

WOLFENBÜTTEL 1.—Herzog August Bibliothek MS 450 (Helmst. 415);
15th century, fols. 1-4 = Stegmüller 74, 4.

WOLFENBÜTTEL 2.—Herzog August Bibliothek MS 3329 (29.7. Aug.); 15th
century, fols. 189-92v.

ZWETTL.—Stiftsbibliothek MS 13; 13th century, parchment, fols. 221v-23
= Eis Z.[74]

3. Slavonic *Vita Adam et Evae*

According to Turdeanu, who follows Nagel, the Slavonic *Vita Adam et
Evae* was translated from a text resembling Nagel's Group II of the Greek
manuscripts (see above, section 1). This group is composed of two
manuscripts, the first of the fifteenth century and the second of the sixteenth. The common features of the Greek and Slavonic texts are: (1) the
penitence and the second temptation of Eve at the same place in the

---

[74]   Stegmüller, 1950, 74.9 mentions a manuscript in Uppsala which is not
       listed by Halford. He also includes two further manuscripts in his
       Supplementum (Madrid: 1976, 8.7ff.) which Halford includes in her list.

order of events, different from that in the other versions;[75] (2) shared omissions, 23:4-26:4 = Slavonic *Vita Adam et Evae* 24; 37:6-39:3 = Slavonic *Vita Adam et Evae* 46. The texts are not identical, and the Slavonic *Vita Adam et Evae* may be said to derive from a text close to this Greek group but not identical with it.

The known manuscripts of this version are only as old as the 14th century and the best edition of it was published with a German translation and commentary by V. Jagič.[76] In addition, a good edition of a variant sixteenth century manuscript was published by Ivanov.[77] This is Sofia, National Library no. 433, pp. 12-20.[78] Both Jagič[79] and Fuchs[80] are of the view that the Slavonic *Vita Adam et Evae* was translated from Greek. Ivanov notes that the oldest manuscript of the fourteenth century claims to have derived from the *Palaea*, but that the Slavonic *Vita Adam et Evae* is not in the Greek *Palaea* nor in the Slavonic *Historical Palaea*.[81]

The Manuscripts

The Slavonic *Vita Adam et Evae* exists in two Slavonic recensions, one long and the other short. The long recension, to which the manuscript published by Jagič also belongs,[82] exists in the following manuscripts:

P   Sofia, National Library, Ms 629, Plovdiv, 16th century.

---

75   See Turdeanu, 1981, 81-82 on all of this. Compare also Denis, *Introduction (2nd ed. unpublished)*. Of course, this incident is now known to exist in all the primary Adam books except for *Apocalypse of Moses*.

76   Jagič, 1893. See review by Schürer, 1893, 398-399. An English translation of the beginning of this work is given by Wells, 1913.

77   Ivanov, 1976, 198-204. See also Turdeanu, 1981, 82.

78   This manuscript is not listed by Turdeanu (see below).

79   Jagič, 1893, 3.

80   Fuchs, 1900, 507.

81   Ivanov, 1976, 206.

82   The text was published by Stojan Novakovic, 1889, 322-427: cf. Stegmüller, 1950, 1.74.15.

belgr.	Belgrade, National Library, Ms 468, Serbian, 14th century.
S	Sofia, National Library, Ms 299, Serbian, 15th century.
m	Vienna, Österreichische Nationalbibliothek, Ms slav. 149, Serbo-Bulgarian, 16th century.
C^1	Sofia, National Library, Ms 509, Serbian with modern Bulgarian forms, 17th century.
n	Belgrade, Academy, Ms 147, 17th-18th century.
AS	Serbian Academy, Ms 470, Serbian, Resava, 17th century.
t	Moscow, Monastery of the Trinity-St. Sergius, No. 7949, 16th century.[83]

According to Turdeanu, the manuscript tradition of the long recension is bifurcate. The oldest direct witness to one group, preserved by the subfamilies P *m* and S *t*, is of the fifteenth century, and the oldest witness to the second group, *belgr. m*, to which the short version is affiliated, is of the same date.[84] In his view grammatical and orthographic features allow the conclusion that the Slavonic *Vita Adam et Evae* was translated in western Macedonia towards the start of the 14th century.[85] Ms *belgr.* appears to be the best single witness.

The second Slavonic recension is abbreviated. It exists in nine manuscripts which fall into three families.

Middle Bulgarian Family

Lo	Loveč (central Bulgaria), second half of 16th century.
H	Bucharest, State Archives, Ms 740, end of 16th century, Moldavian middle-Bulgarian.

---

[83]   This information is all drawn from Turdeanu, 1981, 80-85 who gives many bibliographical details and lists editions, etc. Many of these manuscripts, together with those of the short recension, had been published previously by N.S. Tichonravov, 1863, 1.1-6 and 6-15. Moreover, Stegmüller, 1950, 74.15 also reports that, earlier, two Russian versions were published by Pypin, 1862; some further information is also to be found in Kahana, 1956, 1.3; see also Porfir'ev, 1873, 168-197. Turdeanu, 1981, 437, in an additional note, observes that the unpublished manuscripts are mentioned in the repertory of Jacimirskij, 1921, 1.78-81. Ivanov, 1976, 195-196 mentions some further copies, including Sofia, National Library 681, 15th century, pp. 526-66.

[84]   Turdeanu, 1981, 98-90.

[85]   Turdeanu, 1981, 90-93.

Russian Family

pp	Moscow, Rumjancov Museum, Ms. 358, 15th or 16th century.
pp¹	Moscow, *olim* Rumjancov Museum, Ms. 380, 17th century.
tr	Moscow, Historical Museum, 17th century.
pr	*olim* Kazan, Theological Academy, 17th or 18th century.
pr¹	*olim* Kazan, Theological Academy, 17th or 18th century.

Ukrainian Family

Fr	*olim* collection of priest, Theodore of Dubovec, 17th century.
Fr¹	Manuscript of 1743.[86]

There exist two Roumanian translations of the short Slavonic recension. One survives in three manuscripts of the seventeenth to nineteenth centuries and Turdeanu is of the view that it was made in northern Moldavia in the sixteenth century. The second translation is extant in two manuscripts, one of the eighteenth and the other of the nineteenth century. It is based on the same text-type as the preceding and was probably made in Walachia in the eighteenth century.[87]

Character and Relationships of the Slavonic Vita Adam et Evae

Turdeanu concluded that the short recension of the Slavonic *Vita Adam et Evae* is an abbreviation of a Bulgarian type of text of the long version, made in about the fourteenth century.[88] The views about the char-

---

[86] Turdeanu, 1981, 95-96 gives details of all those manuscripts which have been published. The present location of the manuscripts whose pre-revolutionary location is marked *olim* is presumably unknown. Tichonravov published some manuscripts under a title which may be rendered, Λόγος περὶ ἐξομολογήσεως Εὔας καὶ περὶ νόσου Ἀδάμ· see Tichonravov, 1863, 298-304. Jagič, 1893, 9-17 discusses the relationship between the various witnesses to the long text and the short text. He remarks that his comparison shows that "wenn sie aus älterer Zeit stammten, noch mehr Anknüpfungspunkte für die zweite Redaktion zu gewinnen wären" (p. 14). His fifth chapter is devoted to an analysis of the short recension (pp. 49-58).

[87] Turdeanu, 1981, 104-110.

[88] Turdeanu, 1981, 96-104. He also deals with the division of this recension into subfamilies.

acter of the recensions have varied. Some say that the longer, more
original, recension exhibits the same overall content and order of
material as the Greek *Apocalypse of Moses*, with the addition of some
Christian legends, due to which the general view is that this recension is
Christian.[89] Denis observes that even though the Slavonic is closer to
Greek than to the Latin, it preserves the story of Adam's penitence, not
usually found in Greek.[90] Fuchs too says that in general Slavonic *Vita
Adam et Evae* (referring to the long recension) resembles *Apocalypse
of Moses* in both plot and phraseology, rather than Latin *Vita Adam et
Evae,*[91] while Johnson regards the Slavonic *Vita Adam et Evae* as a version of *Apocalypse of Moses* with Christian interpolations.[92] Nonetheless, it differs from Greek in some places and has certain additions.[93]
Jagič carefully compared his base manuscript with the Greek version,
and drew the conclusions in the fourth chapter of his study. There he
deals with certain passages in which the Slavonic is unique vis-à-vis the
Greek, and explores its relationship in such cases with the Latin version.[94] All these views must now be modified in light of the general
structure exhibited by the Armenian, Georgian and apparently the Coptic works (on the Coptic, see below).

---

[89]   The chief of these additions is the legend of the cheirograph, dealt with
below.

[90]   Denis, 1970, 5; Denis states there that the penitence is also preserved in
Armenian, but he certainly cannot mean the Armenian *Book of Adam*,
which is the translation of *Apocalypse of Moses* and does not have it. At
the time of publication of the first edition of his *Introduction*, he did not
know the Armenian *Penitence of Adam*.

[91]   Fuchs, 1900, 507.

[92]   Johnson, 1985, 250; see above on *Apocalypse of Moses*.

[93]   Jagič, 1893, 17.

[94]   Interestingly, Jagič, 1893 claims that the incident of the Cheirograph of
Adam in chapters 33-34 of the Slavonic derives from Bogomil sources
(pp. 42-43). This view was also espoused by Ivanov, 1976, 208-210. Now
we know the same incident from Armenian texts which cannot be sus-
pected of Bogomil connections: see following section. The matter is discussed in some detail from the Slavonic perspective by Turdeanu, 1981,
44-50.

Johnson quotes the view of Porfir'ev that the work, having originated in Bulgaria and Serbia, moved to Russia, and that it was reworked
under Bogomil influence.[95] According to some authorities, chapters 33-
34, the legend of the cheirograph, are of Bogomil origin, though this
has been contested (see above, note 94). The Slavonic alone of all the
primary Adam books, preserves this story of Satan's second deception
of Adam and Eve and the contract or cheirograph he made with them.
The tale is known, however, in Greek to Georgios Chumnos, in Ethiopic,
in Arabic, and in a variety of Armenian works.[96] It also was current in
Greek and Bulgarian folklore.[97] This legend, in Slavonic circles, relates
that Adam made the contract with Satan either in order to have the
light, or in order to gain the right to work the soil: the latter form of the
legend appears for the first time in the Slavonic *Vita Adam et Evae*.[98]
Its biblical roots seem to be in Colossians 2:14.

The legend has penetrated into religious iconography, as is wit-
nessed by the description of a scene in the *Painter's Manual* of Dionysius of Fourna.[99] In this scene Christ is shown standing, tearing a document written with Hebrew characters, at the end of which is written, τὸ
τοῦ Ἀδὰμ χειρόγραφον. Intriguingly, in Slavonic and Roumanian iconography of recent centuries, a scene of Christ destroying the cheirograph

---

95   Fuchs, 1900, 507; on the general issue of Bogomilism and the pseudepi-
      graphic literature, see Turdeanu, 1981, 1-74. On pp. 43-50 he discusses
      the alleged Bogomil elements in the Slavonic *Vita Adam et Evae*. The lat-
      ter are urged energetically by Ivanov, 1976, 208-210. Ivanov's work dis-
      cusses Bogomil influence on apocryphal literature from a maximalist posi-
      tion.

96   See below, Chapter 4 for further details of this legend. Turdeanu, 1981,
      deals at some length with the connections between the Slavonic *Vita Adam
      et Evae* and the *Legend of the Holy Cross*, which is associated with it in
      the manuscripts (pp. 110-114). The connection between the Adam book
      and the Holy Rood traditions, as was noted above in section 2, also occurs
      in Latin.

97   Turdeanu, 1981, 116. The Greek tale recorded by Megas in Thrace is par-
      ticularly striking: see Megas, 1928, 305-320. This is discussed further be-
      low, Chapter 3, sections 1, 6, and 12.

98   Turdeanu, 1981, 116.

99   Dionysius of Fourna, 5.12.22 (cited in Megas, 1928, 314); Turdeanu, 1981,
      115-122 has discussed the iconography of the contract in detail.

at the time of the Baptism is found.[100] Turdeanu observes that this has
no roots in the Slavonic *Vita Adam et Evae*. He discusses some witnesses to it in the sixteenth century, as well as its spread in iconography.[101] It should be remarked here that this scene exists in a literary
form in Armenian "secondary" Adam texts found in manuscripts dating
from the seventeenth century, which are actually rather older than that.
In view of the wide attestation of this legend, the supposed Bogomil influence may be doubted.

The legend of the wood of the cross is also deeply rooted in the
Slavonic tradition, and is included both in most recensions of Slavonic
Vita Adam et Evae as well as in other Slavonic apocrypha (see Chapter
4, section 10).

4. Armenian *Penitence of Adam*

This work was published by M.E. Stone.[102] The edition was based on
three manuscripts, of fairly late vintage. In general, the work was characterized as "another version of the Adam book, most probably translated
into Armenian from Greek," which "must take its place alongside the
Greek and Latin versions as a major witness to the Adam book. ... The
Penitence of Adam follows a basic story line similar to the *Apocalypse
of Moses* but has the story of the repentance at the beginning." The edi-
tor also concluded that this work may, in some instances, preserve a text
more primitive than the Latin or Greek versions.

The manuscripts are:

A   Jerusalem, Armenian Patriarchate, No. 1458, pp. 380-431, 17th
       century.
B   Jerusalem, Armenian Patriarchate, No. 1370, pp. 127-150, 17th
       century.
C   Erevan, Matenadaran, No. 3461, fols. 66r-87v, dated 1662 C.E.

---

100   See also the comments of Megas, 1928, 317-318 touching on the relation-
       ship of the χειρόγραφον with the Baptism.

101   Turdeanu, 1981, 119-120. Megas, 1928, 314 mentions a painting of Martin
       de Vos which also shows the χειρόγραφον.

102   M.E. Stone, 1981a. Other than the remarks of Mahé mentioned below, the
       Penitence of Adam has not yet been studied.

A certain number of particular points of the Armenian *Penitence of Adam* were investigated in comparison with the Greek and Latin books. Certain of its "special" readings were found to concord with the Greek and Latin works, while others are related to known traditions in other Jewish and Christian sources. Moreover, in chapters 1-9 the search for paradisiacal food is found. In the Armenian *Penitence of Adam* this search is clearly related to food; in the Latin *Vita Adam et Evae* the search is ambiguous, sometimes relating to food and sometimes to repentance.

In one particular *crux interpretationis*, the angel's response to Eve and Seth's search for the oil of the tree of mercy (*Apocalypse of Moses* 13, Latin *Vita Adam et Evae* 42), a most interesting development may be seen. Meyer had observed that the original portion of the Latin *Vita Adam et Evae* is replaced in the present version of this event by the Latin translation of the *Gospel of Nicodemus*. The parallel material in the *Apocalypse of Moses* is apocopated,[103] while the Armenian *Penitence of Adam* produces a version the views of which are strange to say the least. It is conceivable that these differences might provide a diagnostic tool for understanding the *Tendenz* both of the Armenian and of the Greek and Latin versions. Certainly, here is a hint that something unacceptable may have stood in the underlying documents.

This work is closely related to the Georgian *Book of Adam*, which was translated and published after the publication of the Armenian version. J.-P. Mahé made a comparative study of the two and his results are set forth in the next section. Our study to date has uncovered no special relationship between the Armenian *Penitence of Adam* and any of the other numerous Armenian Adam books.

5. Georgian *Book of Adam*

The text of the complete Georgian primary Adam book was published by K'urc'ikidze based on five manuscripts,[104] and her text was trans-

---

[103] M. de Jonge comments: "the text of Greek 13:3-5 in Mss ALCR does not look 'apocopated'," (private communication).

[104] K'urc'ikidze, 1964, 97-136. The existence of this work was noted previously by Džanašvili, 1909, 19-44. Compare also Lüdtke, 1919-20, 157. Mahé, 1981 gives details of the manuscripts in note 8, pp. 227-228.

lated into French by Mahé in 1981.[105] Mahé posited the existence of an
Armenian intermediary for this work, although in private communication he has since indicated that his view on this is not immutable.[106]
Kekelidze, on philological grounds, would place the ancestor of the surviving Georgian manuscripts earlier than the tenth century.[107]

The Georgian manuscripts utilized by K'urc'ikidze are:

Recension α
A   *A 153,* Tbilisi, Institute of Manuscripts, 17th century.
B   *H 433,* Tbilisi, Institute of Manuscripts, 17th century.
C   *H 881,* Tbilisi, Institute of Manuscripts, 17th century.
Q   *K'ut'ais 128,* K'ut'ais, Museum of History and Ethnography, 15-
        16th century.

Recension β
S   *S 5175,* Tbilisi, Institute of Manuscripts, 17th century.[108]

The Georgian *Book of Adam* is much closer to the Armenian
Penitence of Adam than it is to the Greek, Latin and Slavonic primary
Adam books or indeed than it is to the Armenian *Book of Adam* published by Yovsēp'ianc'.[109] The range of contents of the Armenian and
the Georgian primary Adam books is more or less identical. Mahé has
compared the material and reached the following results:

> 1. Armenian, Georgian and Latin go back to a single recension,
> related to Greek manuscripts A, C and L. Latin tends to abbre-
> viate, expand and interpolate, while Georgian and Armenian re-
> main closer to their Greek original. Moreover, where Armenian

---

[105]   Mahé, 1981, 227-260.

[106]   Mahé, 1981, 229. In this he followed the distinguished Georgian scholar, K.
        Kekelidze whose views were presented by Tarchnishvili, 1955, 335-336.

[107]   So reported by Mahé, 1981, 229-230. His argument for a date before 607,
        which was based on the hypothesis of an Armenian intermediary, should
        probably now be abandoned.

[108]   Mahé, 1981, 227-228. He observes the K'urc'ikidze also notes manuscript
        no. 186 of the Georgian Museum of Literature.

[109]   Mahé, 1983, 51-65.

and Georgian diverge, Georgian is generally supported by the Greek or Latin.[110]

2. The Georgian exists in two recensions, α and β: the former surviving in four manuscripts of the seventeenth century and the latter in a single, seventeenth century copy.

3. Kekelidze expressed the view that this Georgian was translated from Greek through the intermediary of a now lost Armenian version.[111] Now that we know the Armenian *Penitence of Adam*, it is clear that the Georgian could not have been translated directly from that work.[112] Possibly that Armenian text of the *Penitence of Adam* is a secondary derivative of an older Armenian version, but in fact, the evidence for an Armenian *Vorlage* of the Georgian is not strong.[113]

6. Fragmentary Coptic Version

1. A parchment fragment of a Coptic version of the primary Adam book was published by W.E. Crum in 1909 from the John Rylands library.[114] This text contains phrases parallel to *Apocalypse of Moses* 31:2, 3, 4, 32:1, 2. Since this passage was not found in the Latin and Slavonic primary Adam books, Crum could compare the Coptic text only with the Greek *Apocalypse of Moses*, Now, however, we have the Armenian and Georgian versions available in addition. Crum notes "considerable differences" between the Coptic and Greek versions, but in a number of these instances the Coptic reads with the Armenian and Georgian against the Greek. Nevertheless, some significant unique readings remain. This fragment seems to have been part of a complete Coptic translation of the primary Adam book, and presumably the same ver-

---

110 Mahé, 1983, 52-53. Thus his earlier assessment in Mahé, 1981, 228-229 has been modified in light of the discovery of the Armenian version.

111 Cited by Mahé, 1981, 229.

112 Mahé, 1983, 53.

113 Mahé, 1983. Because of the textual proximity of the Armenian and Georgian versions, Mahé suggests a series of corrections to each, on the basis of the other: 53-64.

114 Crum, 1909, no. 84, p. 40.

sion was utilized by the Timothy of Alexandria in his *Discourse on Abbatôn* (see next paragraph). It contained the penitence material, and its text in other ways may have resembled Armenian and Georgian and less closely Greek.

2. Crum, in a note to his publication of the Rylands library fragment of 1909, refers to another fragment, this one in Berlin. It was published earlier, in 1904, by Leipoldt from a papyrus sheet.[115] Denis describes this "le texte ... paraphrasé de *Ad. Ev.* 28-29."[116]

3. Murdoch drew attention to apocryphal Adam traditions in *Discourse on Abbatôn* attributed to the fourth-century Timothy, Bishop of Alexandria.[117] The text itself was published and translated by E. A. Wallis Budge and similarities to the Adam books are quite striking.[118]. It seems very likely to us that this sermon is dependent on the primary Adam work and if it is a genuine work of Timothy of the fourth century, then it is exceedingly important for establishing a *terminus ad quem* of the primary Adam books, and also for the dating of the Coptic version. Intriguingly, the superscription of the text relates that it was found by Timothy in the "Library of Jerusalem" on occasion of a pilgrimage. The question of the authenticity of the attribution and dating of the Coptic document must be examined carefully, however, as well as the extent and exact character of its relationship to the primary Adam books.

---

[115] Leipoldt, 1904, 1.172.

[116] Denis, *Introduction (2nd ed. unpublished)*.

[117] Murdoch, 1973, 162-163. This material is referred to in further detail by A. van Lantschoot, 1947, 260-268.

[118] Budge, 1914. In that book, on page 483 we find a reworking of the story of the rebellion of Satan (called Abbatôn) by his refusal to bow down to Adam. This is rather similar to the material in the primary Adam books as is that on p. 485 relating to the seduction of Eve. Particularly notable is Satan's reproach to Adam outside the Garden which seems to be composed of phrases found in Chapters 12-16 of the Latin, Armenian and Georgian works.

4. Burmester pointed out the use of the Coptic Adam book in *The Mysteries of the Apostle John and of the Holy Virgin*.[119]

5. Another probable witness to the Coptic version is to be found in two Arabic leaves from the Coptic monastery of St. Pishoi.[120]

---

[119]   Burmester, 1938, 356-357 proposed that the story in this work about Adam and Eve, although containing some Coptic elements, is ultimately based on the primary Adam writings.

[120]   Burmester, 1975, 305, 17. Troje, 1916 wrote an extensive study of representations of Adam and Eve in Paradise in a fresco from the fourth century necropolis of El Bagauat, close by the Great Oasis near Libyan desert (5-6). In this fresco the serpent may be seen hanging over the wall of the Garden. In his discussion he claims that a form of Adam legend like that in *Apocalypse of Moses* 16 lies behind this representation (p. 8). However, he observes that the tree represented together with snake is a vine, therefore the present form of the Adam book is not involved (p. 9). If the dating is reliable, this fresco is a very early witness to the presence of a developed Adam legend in the Egyptian area.

CHAPTER 2

THE CHIEF CRITICAL AND LITERARY ISSUES OF
THE PRIMARY ADAM BOOKS

As one surveys what has been written about the chief critical issues of
the primary Adam books, three major interconnected complexes may
be noted. The first has to do with the provenance of the Adam books,
the second with their date and the third with their original language. Are
the primary Adam books Jewish or Christian? To this issue is related the
second question, about original language. If the original language was
Hebrew or Aramaic, then it becomes extremely likely that the books are
of Jewish origin. If the original language was Greek, the decision about
provenance must be made on grounds other than that of language. As
for date: if the date is pre-Christian, then the books are Jewish; if the
date is post-Christian, then the decision about that too must be made
on other grounds. It is logical, therefore, to examine first of all the arguments for the original language of the primary Adam books, then arguments for the date and finally, arguments relating Jewish or Christian
provenance which are not dependent on the original language or date.

A *caveat* should be issued at this point. The present work claims
only to present what has been said about the Adam books, and to do so
in a fashion that will help clarify the issues and set the agenda. Certain
preliminary evaluations will be offered, but in this we do not claim to be
even partially exhaustive. As noted in the Introductory Remarks to the
volume, there is one exception to this approach. The specific linguistic
and textual arguments for a Semitic original have been reassessed by
Gideon Bohak and myself and our results are given in an Excursus included in the present chapter.

1. Original Language of the Primary Adam Books

It is generally accepted that Latin *Vita Adam et Evae,* Slavonic *Vita
Adam et Evae,* Armenian *Penitence of Adam,* and Georgian *Life of
Adam* were translated from Greek.[1] This seems most likely to be true of

---

1   Concerning the Georgian, see above Chapter 1, section 5.9.

the Coptic version as well, though it has been little studied. The first question to be posed, then, is whether the present Greek form of the *Apocalypse of Moses*, or for that matter the Greek *Vorlage* of some other of the primary Adam works, was originally written in Greek or whether it was translated into Greek from a Semitic language. One common hypothesis is that *Apocalypse of Moses* was translated from a Semitic original and that the other works somehow derive from it. Another form of this hypothesis maintains that there existed a Jewish Semitic Adam book which underlies all of the present primary Adam writings and that the *Apocalypse of Moses* too is a reworked document based on that Semitic Adam book.[2]

In the case of both these hypotheses, the method by which a Semitic original was detected was identical. Scholars sought Semitisms in the text of *Apocalypse of Moses* (and in the case of the second hypothesis, sometimes in the Latin *Vita Adam et Evae*) which supposedly derived from the Semitic original. The plausibility of these claims depends on whether the instances adduced are compelling on textual and linguistic grounds and not on which of the above two views about the relationship of the documents a given scholar adopted. That literary question is a quite different one, to be approached in other ways as will be made evident below.

Many scholars simply declared that there was a Semitic original, but offered no exact or detailed argumentation to prove it. Extreme examples of such unsupported assertions are the claims that the study of the Greek *Apocalypse of Moses* leaves no doubt that the original language of the work was Aramaic (C.C. Torrey), or that the Adam book "is an Aramaic work, written during the first century A.D., which has survived in Latin and Greek manuscripts" (H.T. Andrews).[3] Charlesworth

---

2   Meyer, 1878, 198-206 regards the Latin *Vita Adam et Evae* as more original, particularly in its plusses, than the Greek *Apocalypse of Moses*. Compare also Levison, 1988, 25.

3   Torrey, 1945, 133; Andrews, 1964, 73. Similarly Forsyth, 1987, states quite unambiguously that the Latin *Vita Adam et Evae* and *Apocalypse of Moses* are "divergent redactions, in Latin and Greek respectively, of a common Hebrew or Aramaic original" (p. 227). No demonstrations of this assertion are offered and Forsyth seems quite unconscious of the existence of any other forms of the primary Adam writing than the Greek and Latin. He assumes the existence of an original Hebrew or Aramaic

speaks of wide agreement about a Semitic original[4] and Denis says that
the Adam book was composed in Greek liberally paraphrasing Hebrew
or Aramaic source documents (p. 7).[5] Schäfer also speaks of a Hebrew
Grundschrift, from which the Greek, Latin and Slavonic primary Adam
works derive.[6] It is, by the way, a strange fact that no arguments at all
have been put forward in the scholarly literature even attempting to
show that the original was Aramaic rather than Hebrew, or vice versa.

The first serious consideration of the original language was
conducted by Fuchs.[7] He grants that there are a few points at which
Greek seems to be implied, chief among which are ἀχερουσία λίμνη and
the word play ἔλαιον τοῦ ἐλέου, as well as the use of LXX. Nonetheless,
he holds for a Hebrew original, giving a number of examples, most of
which were later taken over by Kahana who also attempted to reconstruct the Hebrew original. All Fuchs' examples, like those of Kahana,
are discussed in the Excursus at the end of this section. A third attempt
to prove a Semitic original was made by Sharpe in his thesis, details of
which were quoted by Johnson.[8] Johnson concludes:

> Although no Hebrew text is extant, it is most probable that there
> did exist an original Hebrew document or documents from
> which the *Apocalypse* and the *Vita* were translated, the Greek di-

---

"Book of Adam" which was the source of these two works and of the
Apocalypse of Adam from Nag Hammadi. This latter work he attributes to
the first century B.C.E. with no serious supporting argumentation.

4   Charlesworth, 1981, 74: so also Bamberger, 1962, 1.44-45.

5   To be fair, neither Charlesworth nor Denis, because of the character of
     their works, may have felt it necessary to adduce detailed proofs. Of
     course, an exhaustive search of various encyclopedias, dictionaries, and
     the like could lengthen this list very considerably. That is superfluous.
     Below, in section 4, the supposed relationship between the literary history
     of the book(s) of Adam and the language of its *Vorlage* is discussed. It is
     an argument that is not convincing.

6   Schäfer, 1977, 425-426. His article provides additional material on the
     rabbinic Adam traditions.

7   Fuchs, 1900, 511.

8   Sharpe, 1969, 116-139 [*non vidi*] cited by Johnson, 1985, 250-251.

rectly from the Hebrew and the Latin directly either from the Hebrew or from the Greek.[9]

In spite of this, in Fuchs' footsteps, Johnson notes that the author was familiar with the Septuagint of Genesis 1-5 and that Lake Acheron in *Apocalypse of Moses* 37:3 derives from Hellenistic sources.

Lachs ingeniously formulated a number of Hebrew reconstructions, allegedly designed to clarify difficulties encountered in the Latin and Greek primary Adam books. On this basis, he put forward the claim that the book was originally written in Hebrew. His argument does not hold water, for reasons set forth in the Excursus at the end of this section.[10]

A dissenting view is that of Sparks in *Apocryphal Old Testament*. He says that no sound evidence for Semitic original has been adduced and that the presence of Greek terms and expressions unlikely to be found in a translation mitigates against it, as does the fact that the references to the Old Testament are to the LXX.[11] A similar position is taken by Bertrand, who admits a "Judaeo-Greek" original, and tries to show that none of the arguments made for a Hebrew original are truly convincing.[12] The view of Schürer-Vermes-Millar is substantially the same.[13]

The "Hebraisms" that have been adduced are susceptible to evaluation, using the tools developed in the study of Judeo-Greek texts since the period of Fuchs, to discover whether they prove that the primary Adam books (or their putative source) were written in Hebrew. In

---

9   Johnson, 1985, 251.

10   See Lachs, 1982, 172-176. Many Hebrew reconstructions had already been proposed by Neumark, 1910, 1.307-312. However his reconstructions are quite impressionistic and he does not argue closely from them.

11   Sparks, 1984, 142.

12   Bertrand, 1987a, 26-28. Turdeanu, 1981, 75 talks of a Greek Christian redaction of largely pre-Christian material.

13   Schürer-Vermes-Millar, 1987, 3.2, 759.

[handwritten annotations: "Earliest text is in Greek", "no proof of Hebrew original"]

the Excursus which follows, research carried out by Gideon Bohak in collaboration with the writer is presented. Our conclusion is that the arguments adduced so far do not demonstrate that the original was Hebrew or Aramaic. This does not prove that the book was written in Greek, but it does establish securely that the arguments adduced so far for its Semitic origin are not conclusive.

Excursus

G.Bohak and M.E.Stone

The Arguments Adduced For a Semitic Original

As observed above, detailed arguments for a Hebrew original of the book were first put forth by Fuchs, were largely repeated by Kahana, while a number of additional considerations were brought into play by Sharpe, followed by Johnson. Here we shall examine the chief arguments in detail, to attempt to see whether they are compelling.

'Ιαήλ יה אל - (Fuchs; Kahana). This is clearly a Hebrew name, the result of the combination of two divine names, יה and אל. It appears twice as an address to God, in 29:4 and 33:5. The two names are among those "which should not be erased" (b. Shebu'ot 35a). 'Ιαήλ occurs in many texts as an angelic name.[14] However, it should be stressed that the mere appearance of a Hebrew name does not have any bearing on the original language of the text, for names, particularly divine and angelic ones, were often borrowed from one language to another. 'Ιαήλ is no more or less convincing in this context than Μιχαήλ or Γαβριήλ or any other name which could produce the angelic name 'Ιαήλ.

---

[14] This is also true of the Slavonic *Vita Adam et Evae* corresponding to *Apocalypse of Moses* 29:4. It occurs as an angelic name e.g. in *Sefer HaRazim* (Second Firmament 140), in *Bibl. Ant.* 26:12, and in *Apoc. Abr.* 10:4, 9. Note also its occurrence as a magical name in Preisendanz, *Papyri Graeci Magici* 4.3033. An orthographically identical name is the Greek form of Jael (Hebrew יעל) in Judges 4-5.

'Αλληλούια הללויה - (Fuchs; Kahana). This is cited as evidence of a transcription. However, it early became a common expression in writings not composed in Hebrew but in Greek. Lampe, vol. 1, p. 75, cites the frequent appearance of ἀλληλούια in hymns, doxologies etc. which were originally written in Greek (not translated). This was already known to Eusebius, who says (*Comm. in Is.* 19.18)[15] that because Hebrew words such as 'Αλληλούια, ἀμήν, σαβαώθ and others appear in the Holy Bible, they have entered the Church's (Greek) language.

ὀργῆς υἱός in 3:2 is cited by Fuchs and Kahana as a literal translation of a Hebraism. The two verses they cite as parallels, Prov 17:25 and Ephes 2:3, do not seem to prove the case: Prov 17:25 reads ὀργὴ πατρὶ υἱὸς ἄφρων and the Hebrew has the same sense, while Ephes 2:3 does not have the exact expression, nor do we see how, even if the exact expression occurred in Ephesians, it would strengthen the argument for a Hebrew original. As for the expression itself, it should be noted that υἱὸς ὀργῆς would have been a perfect Semitism (cf. Liddell, Scott and Jones, 1961, *s.v.* υἱός 4, and examples such as υἱὸς ἀδικίας [2 Samuel 7:10] and υἱὸς θανατώσεως [1 Samuel 26,16]).[16] However, the inverted word-order (כעס ⟶ בן) is impossible in a Semitic language, and is best explained as the result of a Greek speaker's attempt to use a "Hebraistic" idiom or (not plausible here) as a corruption in the manuscripts.[17] A Greek speaker might not have known that υἱὸς ὀργῆς is a "good" Hebraism and ὀργῆς υἱός is not.

---

[15] Ziegler, 1975, 132.

[16] See also υἱὸς θανάτου in 1 Sam 20:31 and in 2 Sam 12:5.

[17] In fact, the reverse order, υἱὸς ὀργῆς is recorded by Nagel in two Mss, his Br and S[1] (Bertrand's Q and Z) which are secondary members of his Family III. Of course, one cannot assume any sort of corruption in the original on the basis of this sort of argument nor do these two manuscripts provide any support for an emendation. In further detail, see note 24 below, which implies additional nuancing of the statement made here. Conceivably, of course, an initial "correct" order could have been reversed here in all witnesses. The reading of Q and Z would then be a second transposition.

ζῇ ὁ θεός (18:1 Fuchs; Kahana) – This is supposed to reflect Hebrew חי אלהים. Indeed, Hatch and Redpath record this phrase in
Amos 8:14, though the expression ζῇ ὁ κύριος is much more common. Lampe quotes the following from 1 Clem. 58.2 ζῇ γὰρ ὁ θεὸς
καὶ ζῇ ὁ κύριος Ἰησοῦς Χριστός.[18] This shows that the biblical expression had migrated into works that were composed in Greek.

λόγοι παρανομίας דברי בליעל (Fuchs: Kahana 21:2) – This is a
Hebraism and the expression does not occur in the dictionaries.
A check of the *TLG* database turned up no truly comparable instance. This sort of construction, dubbed an "adjectival genitive"
or a "genitive of quality" is well-known in New Testament Greek.[19]

ἰδοὺ ἐγώ הנני (41:1 Fuchs; Kahana) – The expression is common
in the LXX, of course, but also occurs regularly in the New Testament, e.g. Mat 10:16, 11:10, Acts 9:21; etc. This implies that, even if
it started as a literal translation of Hebrew, it quickly migrated to
works originally composed in Greek.

ἐν τῷ φυλάσσειν ἡμᾶς (15:2) ἐν τῷ γινώσκειν (18:3) –
This type of expression might be a Hebraism, but is also not unknown in normal Greek: all the evidence is discussed by N.
Turner.[20] Furthermore Turner observes, "the construction ἐν τῷ
with inf. occurs... often in Lk-Ac... it occurs in the papyri occasion-
ally, but this expression... belongs almost exclusively to Bibl.
Greek, through the influence of Hebrew."[21] Moreover, Mayser
cites examples of this usage from Greek papyri (e.g. ἐν τῷ
παραπορεύεσθαι τὸν βασιλέα).[22] In addition, the example in 15:2

---

[18]   Jaubert, 1971, 192-193 comments on this phrase, "tournure empruntée à
       l'Ancien Testament, sans doute sous influence liturgique ... et appliquée
       ici à une formule trinitaire."

[19]   Turner, 1976, 48-49.

[20]   Turner, 1976, 8; on pp. 144-5 he discusses the evidence.

[21]   Turner, 1976, 8.

[22]   Compare Mayser, 1926, 2.238-239. See also the remarks of Soisalon-
       Soininen, 1965, 81.

ἐγένετο ἐν τῷ φυλάσσειν ὑμᾶς, is another example of a "wrong Hebraism." To be a true Hebraism, it should have read καὶ ἐγένετο etc. reflecting the Hebrew ויהי. Without the καὶ it cannot be a Hebraism, but is probably a "misuse" of a Hebraism.

ῥῆμα ἐν ᾧ (16:1 Fuchs; Kahana) – This is good Greek and does not require the assumption of a Hebraism.

ξύλον ἐν ᾧ ῥέει (9:3; 13:2) – The syntax is good Greek. As for the "Hebraistic" usage of ξύλον for "tree," this is attested in many works originally composed in Greek.[23] It is interesting to note that the author uses both ξύλον and δένδρον for the word "tree," and the same phenomenon is found in the LXX.

Hebrew error – One supposed Hebrew error has been detected, the confusion of ה and ח: בחבלים meaning "with/in ropes" having been confused with בהבלים ἐν ματαίοις (25:1). This is possible, but not necessarily correct. It should be noted that the next verse mentions τῶν ὀδύνων, the usual equivalent of חבלים.[24]

ἰός = ראש and κεφάλη = ראשית (19:3).[25] The suggestion that ἰός translates Hebrew ראש and that the putative Hebrew had a word-play on ראש and ראשית, a pun lost in the Greek translation, seems very tempting at first blush. It should, however, be observed that the equation ἰός = ראש is not very probable. The word ראש or רש meaning "poison" occurs twelve times in the Hebrew Bible, but the Greek Bible never translates it ἰός and its common equivalents

---

23   Lampe, *s.v.*

24   Note that the issue is exegetical here; Bertrand, 1987a, in his text accepts the reading καμάτοις. It is typical of the problems of this edition that he does not note explicitly that this is the reading of a single manuscript, Nagel's AT, i.e. Ms L, a 16th century member of Family I. In his introduction, in characterizing L, Bertrand speaks of its occasional "lections meilleures" but it is this very instance in 25:1 that he cites.

25   See Schürer, 1909, 3.288-9. Kaufmann, 1932, 1.789 refers to Hebraisms (quoting Fuchs, 1900, 511-2) and notes that Neumark has made many retroversions (2.307-8): see note 10 above.

are χολή and θυμός.[26] It should also be noted that the Greek word ἰός fits the context admirably, since one of its meanings is "poison, as of serpents" (Liddell-Scott-Jones, 1961, *s.v.*). In general, Hebrew retroversions should be sought at points at which the Greek text makes poor sense. A very convincing proof is required for contexts, like the present, in which the Greek is quite comprehensible. Thus the present example is judged unconvincing in particular and on general grounds.

In an article published in 1982, S.T. Lachs proposes a Hebrew original on the basis of a number of points at which he argues that a retroversion into Hebrew clarifies obscurities of the Greek or Latin texts.[27] These instances are all ingenious, but in our judgment none is compelling in itself, as can be seen by examining each of his suggestions closely :

1) 'Αμιλαβές (1:3) – Lachs suggests that this is a corruption of a Hebrew nick-name מעילוני לבש, and that this name was supposed to stand in contrast to ἀδιαφωτός, "one devoid of light". This suggestion is extremely improbable for מעילוני לבש is very poor Hebrew, if it is Hebrew at all. Moreover, the interpretation of such a hypothetical nick-name as referring to the midrashic interpretation of Adam and Eve's garments (כתנות אור instead of כתנות עור), but using the word מעיל instead of כתנת, seems unlikely.

2) In Latin *Vita Adam et Evae* 18:1 Lachs interprets *a lumine vitae istius* by assuming that this Latin text reflects a partial mistranslation of Hebrew חייך as an oath (which he renders "by your life"). This implies two errors. First, that the translator missed the syntactic role of חייך. Second, that he mistook מזרח ("from the east") for "from the light of." Yet the Latin text says "from the light of this (*istius*) life," and not "from the light of your life." Moreover, (*contra* Lachs, note 11) the idiom "light of (this) life" sounds very

---

[26]   The Rabbinic texts which contain parallels to this narrative detail never call the serpent's poison or sperm ראש or זוהמא, e.g. *b. Shabbat* 146a. For further examples, see Ginzberg, 1928, 5.123-4, 133-4.

[27]   Lachs,1982, 172-176.

plausible in light of Job 33:30, and especially Ps 56:14 "that I may walk before God in the light of life,"[28]

3) ἐκ τῶν ζιζανίων τοῦ Ἀδάμ (16:3) Lachs proposes that this derives from Hebrew מ(ז)וני אדמה ("from the tares of the earth") erroneously translated as מ(ז)וני אדם ("from the tares of Adam").[29] Lachs correctly states that the Devil's argument at this point is not very clear, and that contrasting "tares of the earth" with "the fruit of Paradise" might sound better than contrasting "tares of Adam" with that fruit. However, we know that Adam guarded that part of Paradise where the male animals were (15:3). He would therefore have been in charge of the snake (ὁ ὄφις). Lachs' emendation is not really necessary, since the text makes sense as it now stands.[30]

These ingenious suggestions do not prove that the book was originally written in Hebrew. This is true too of more general phenomena sometimes cited, such as the examples given by Sharpe (quoted by Johnson) of Hebraistic syntax and style, including consistent parataxis and the verb preceding the subject. All these phenomena are well known to students of New Testament Greek and none of them can serve as a criterion to prove that a text was translated into Greek rather than composed in a biblicizing Greek.

---

28   So the NRSV. The Septuagint understood אור החיים not as "light of life" but as "light of the living," yet the idiom could obviously have been understood both ways.

29   Lachs does not mention it, but his retroversion assumes that καὶ τῆς γυναικὸς αὐτοῦ is a later addition, and should be omitted (as in ms. C), otherwise the retroversion, "the tares of the earth, and of his wife," makes no sense at all.

30   A further suggestion of Lachs' is that in 19:1 the Greek ἤνοιξα δέ is a mistranslation of a Hebrew ואפתה לו "and I was seduced by him" as ואפתח לו "and I opened for him." Quite apart from the fact that this sort of use of a dative pronoun after פתח is not to be found in the Hebrew Bible, the Greek manuscripts do not provide strong support for the presence of the pronoun. It is found only in Mss ATL (so Nagel). Moreover, the text makes perfectly good sense as it stands.

The purpose of all our discussion is not to prove that the book was originally composed in Greek. It is simply to assess the plausibility of those arguments that have been adduced in the past to prove that it was composed in Hebrew. From our examination of the data, however, it clearly emerges that so far the search for specific proofs that the Greek text was translated from a Hebrew original has proved futile. The text is full of (indeed it is foul with) Hebraisms; this is apparent throughout. The central question should be: what do all these Hebraisms mean? Are they necessarily all the result of translation from a Semitic original or might they be the result produced by an author writing Greek, but trying to "biblicize" his language?[31]

If the hypothesis of a translation is to be entertained, it would imply a rather free translation, because many Greek forms in the text cannot be the result of a stereotypic or servile translation from a Semitic language, whereas they conform with later Greek usage.[32] The very "free" character of the putative translation, however, would make demonstration that the text was translated from Hebrew a very difficult undertaking.

A further direction of investigation which might perhaps be pursued is the existence in the book of "bad" Hebraisms, that is forms of expression which may have seemed Hebraistic to a Greek speaker, but do not in fact conform precisely to the phraseology encountered in texts which are known to have been translated from a Hebrew original.[33]

To sum up this discussion, it should be emphasized that despite the efforts of many scholars, we do not yet have tools to determine whether a text was composed in Greek or whether it was translated into Greek from a Semitic original. The question is extremely difficult, and many complicating factors are involved,

---

[31] Kraft has proposed that we even consider "the possibility of a speaker of (semi-) Hebraized Greek!"

[32] This subject should be looked into more deeply than is possible here.

[33] Such an investigation will be hampered by the revisions and corruptions which the manuscripts have suffered. It should still be possible.

historical, linguistic and above all textual. Moreover, the examination of specific works on their own is may not be the most promising approach to the problem. A serious investigation should perhaps begin with an attempt to classify all the Greek Apocrypha and Pseudepigrapha according to their linguistic characteristics, in order to isolate those that were certainly written in Greek on the one side, and those that were certainly translated from a Semitic source on the other. Only then might it be possible to make any significant comments on those works which remain somewhere in the middle – to which category the *Apocalypse of Moses* almost certainly belongs.

2. Date of the Primary Adam Writings

The question of the date of the primary Adam writings is not less important than that of the original language. The arguments that have been developed so far in order to fix the date of these writings may be divided into two types. One type of argument starts from the extant writings and attempts to establish dates *ante quem* for them on literary, codicological, philological or other grounds. In general such arguments, as we shall show, lead to a date in the first centuries C.E., probably before 400 C.E. The other approach seeks arguments from the content of the primary Adam writings to establish their time of composition. One such argument is based on a supposed reference to Herod's temple, while the others attempt to place the primary Adam writings in the historical development of certain ideas or concepts.

Literary, Codicological and Philological Arguments

On philological and codicological grounds Meyer argued that :

a. Ms P of the Latin *Vita Adam et Evae* came from an original of 730-740 C.E.
b. The original Adam book must be older than the later Christian Adam books.
c. Parts of *Apocalypse of Moses* were known to the author of the *Gospel of Nicodemus*.

Therefore, he concludes, the primary Adam writings, which he calls the
first Christian translations of the original Adam book, must be no later
than 500 C.E. and are consequently earlier.[34] The same arguments (b.
and c. in particular) were also adduced by Bertrand.[35] He is quite con-
vinced that, in spite of the complex relations between *Apocalypse of
Moses* and the *Gospel of Nicodemus*, the latter is dependent on the
former and he attempts to show that by arguments based on the texts
themselves.[36]

Meyer's argument (a) only enables us to date the Latin *Vita
Adam et Evae* to earlier than the eighth century,[37] but more is to be
learned from his argument (b). One of the secondary Adam books with
best claims to antiquity is *Cave of Treasures*.[38] Although the date of the
present form of *The Cave of Treasures* is under some discussion, Götze

---

[34] Meyer, 1878, 205-06, 218; Johnson, 1985, 252. Meyer also argues (d) that
      the story of the fall of Satan was known to Mohammed, thus implying a
      seventh century date, and also that (e) Armenian and Slavonic are transla-
      tions of Greek. Neither of these latter arguments takes the date back any
      further than do others he has adduced, nor is argument (d) particularly
      convincing.

[35] Bertrand, 1987a, 29.

[36] Bertrand, 1987a, 63-64. Moreover, Bertrand raises another type of argu-
      ment: the possibility that certain early Christian texts utilized traditions
      found in *Apocalypse of Moses*, although he cautiously determines that so
      far dependence on *Apocalypse of Moses* by any such source cannot be
      proved. The texts that he discusses include *The Protoevangelium of
      James*, 13:1; Irenaeus, *adv. haer*, 3.23.5; *demonst.* 16; Tertullian, *de pati-
      entia* 5:7.10.15; *paenit.* 2:3; 12:9. A similar argument is advanced by
      Schultz, 1978, 163-166, 185-189. He suggests three themes in which Ire-
      naeus draws upon the primary Adam books: the "strokes" that God laid
      upon Adam; the serpent as Satan's "instrument"; and the reason for
      Satan's jealousy of humans. The problem with the use of these depen-
      dencies for dating is that they are not close enough to demonstrate the
      existence of a text substantially resembling the primary Adam books at
      the time of Irenaeus, but only perhaps of a document or of traditions
      similar to them in some way.

[37] This date is also suggested by some palaeographic criteria invoked by
      Mozley: see above, Chapter 1, section 2.

[38] See below, Chapter 4, section 3 on this work.

would see it at least as dating from prior to 500 C.E. Moreover, his view that the present form of the book derives from an earlier form of *Cave of Treasures* (which he dubs *Urschatzhöhle*) which is of the fourth century has been generally accepted.[39] Su-Min Ri would argue in addition that the sources of *The Cave of Treasures* existed from the third century, from the period before the creation of the Pešiṭta.[40] Denis argues that "le noyau primitif a été daté aussi au 4ᵉ s., comme l'oeuvre d'un judéo-chrétien antijuif, peut-être ébionite."[41]

Since *Cave of Treasures* is admitted to be dependent on the primary Adam writings, the latter must have existed before the mid- or even the early fourth century.[42] Furthermore, the dependence of the *Gospel of Nicodemus* on the primary Adam books indicates a date as old or older than does the dependence of the *Cave of Treasures* on them.[43] This line of investigation has not been pursued further, and it seems likely that additional careful study of these literary relationships of the primary Adam writings will prove fruitful.

Above, in Chapter 1, section 6 we discussed the likely dependence of the *Discourse on Abbatôn* attributed to Timothy, Archbishop of Alexandria (ca. 380-385) on the primary Adam writing. If this depen-

---

[39]   So already Bezold, 1888, x. Götze, 1922, 1-92. This view is also accepted by Brock, as noted in Chapter 4, section 3 and by Su-Min Ri, 1987, 487.xviii.

[40]   Su-Min Ri, 1987, 487.xxii-xxiii.

[41]   Denis, *Introduction (2nd ed. manuscript)*.

[42]   Similar dates are quoted by Charlesworth, 1981, 91. However, the whole question of the exact relationship between the various primary Adam books and *The Cave of Treasures* should be examined once more. Perhaps more precision is possible than has been achieved so far. Götze does not throw any particular light on this problem.

[43]   The *Grundschrift*, at least, of *Gospel of Nicodemus* is referred to by Epiphanius, *adv. Haer.* 50.1 and so existed in ca. 375, while the preface of the present Greek version goes back to 425 C.E. There is no basis for the date 360 for the Armenian Adam books given by Wells, 1913, 126 and Kahana, 1956, [2], quoting Preuschen, 1900. The Armenian language was not even written at that time.

dance is verified by further careful examination and, moreover, if the attribution of the *Discourse on Abbatôn* is confirmed (perhaps the more difficult of the two tasks), then a convincing criterion will have emerged for the dating of a form of the primary Adam writings which includes the full penitence tradition to the fourth century C.E. or earlier.

Internal Criteria for Dating

From within the book, only one specific dating criterion has been proposed. This is that "since the existence of the Herodian Temple seems to be presupposed" a date between 20 B.C.E. and C.E. 70 is indicated.[44] The alleged reference to the Herodian Temple is in Latin *Vita Adam et Evae* 29:4-10. Yet is should be noted that this passage, which is found only in the Latin *Vita Adam et Evae* and not in the Greek *Apocalypse of Moses*, is Christian in its present form and can be made Jewish only by a process of excision. Moreover, even if this passage were Jewish, as Bertrand, following Nagel, judiciously comments, it refers to the eschatological temple and is, therefore, no indication of dating.[45]

Fuchs, followed by Wells, argued that certain ideas in the primary Adam writings are related to *2 Enoch* and that this relationship shows an early date. Wells adds that the author of the document underlying *Apocalypse of Moses* moved in the same circles as the author of *2 Enoch* and as St. Paul.[46] This remains to be demonstrated. Bertrand daringly (but as a last resort) attempts to use the ideas of the book as a criterion for date and concludes that the book is later than ben Sira and *Jubilees*, but probably earlier than St. Paul.[47] He would thus come down

---

[44]   Eissfeldt, 1965, 637. This position is also taken by Torrey, 1945, 133 and Denis, 1970, 6. It was introduced into the discussion by Bousset and was also accepted by Beer, 1905, 264. It is also the view of Bamberger, 1962, 1.45. who claims that this date also fits the concept of Satan as a fallen angel. Sharpe, 1973, 35 asserts a date in the first century B.C.E. with no supporting argumentation.

[45]   Bertrand, 1987a, 29. See already Turdeanu, 1981, 75, quoting Nagel, 1974.

[46]   Wells, 1913, 126, 130.

[47]   Bertrand, 1987a, 30-31. Sharpe, 1973, argues that "The Jewish concept of Adam as the source of sin and the hope of salvation, as described in the

for a date of between 100 B.C.E. and 50 CE. This whole endeavour is methodologically suspect.

Other arguments, also about the conceptual or ideological "fit" of the book, leave as much to be desired. Thus, in support for a date before the destruction of the Temple, Denis adds the observations that the book contains nothing anti-Christian and that its view of Judaism is pre-Rabbinic. Here there is a hidden assumption that Jewish works composed after the destruction, when the Christian and Jewish communities split, must bear a polemical, anti-Christian character. Yet, there exist works that contain nothing anti-Christian, but nonetheless were written by Jews after the destruction, as the instance of 4 Ezra graphically illustrates. The category of "pre-Rabbinic" was introduced into the discussion already by Wells, although neither Wells nor Denis explains what it means.[48] The Adam book, if it was Jewish, is not part of Rabbinic literature: that is obvious. What is not clear is that this means that it is pre-Rabbinic rather than just non-Rabbinic. Were no Jewish works written after the first century except those appertaining to the tradition of Rabbinic Judaism?

We propose considering another form of the *argumentum e silentio* which stresses not the absence of anti-Christian polemic, but the absence of any Christian references, particularly from those points in the narrative of Adam and Eve which played a central role in the Christian economy of salvation. We might regard this as a possible indication of the Jewish character of the work. This consideration gains some weight in view of the fact that nearly all the primary Adam writings show some secondary, clearly Christian, intervention in the archangel's eschatological prophecy given to Seth and Eve at the Garden gate (*Apocalypse of Moses* 13; Latin *Vita Adam et Evae* 42 and parallels). Moreover, the handling of the same narrative Adam material in the clearly Christian writings such as *Cave of Treasures* or the Armenian *Cycle of Four Works* provides a striking contrast. This absence of ex-

---

Apoc. Mos., is of the same theological circle as that of St. Paul's doctrine of sin and salvation" (p. 36). In an older article, Kabisch argued that the date of *Apocalypse of Moses* could be fixed by assessing the relationship of its ideas to those of 4 Ezra and Paul. Its idea of the evil heart is older than 4 Ezra while the idea of the third heaven seemed to him to point to the time of Paul: see Kabisch, 1905, 132-34.

48   Wells, 1913, 126; Denis, 1970, 6.

plicit Christian references is not a proof of Jewish origin, but it is a factor that should be brought into account in characterizing the book.

Sparks, ever judicious, simply says that the Adam book was written most probably in the first to third centuries C.E. in Greek using extant Jewish traditions. It is unknown whether the book was written by a Jew or a Christian.[49]

3. Provenance

Those arguments which claim that the primary Adam writings or their underlying source are Jewish, and which do not depend upon either original language or date, seem to end up listing the ideas or traditions in the primary Adam books for which there are good Jewish parallels, either in the Apocrypha and Pseudepigrapha or in Rabbinic literature. There are variations in presentation. Sometimes the argument is made on the basis of slightly censored forms of the surviving primary Adam writings and on other occasions on the basis of their putative source document. In neither case are these arguments compelling in themselves.[50] In order for an argument of this type to be convincing, what is required are not just parallels between the primary Adam books and Jewish writings, but instances of parallels between the primary Adam books and Jewish writings which can exist *only* in Jewish writings. Otherwise, the parallels can always be construed as reflecting Jewish material that has migrated into Christian documents or transmission.

Let us give some examples. J. Kaufmann, in the German *Encyclopädia Judaica* declares that the three works *Apocalypse of Moses,* Latin *Vita Adam et Evae,* and Slavonic *Vita Adam et Evae* are all Jewish with slight Christian reworking.[51] He lists the following Jewish features:

---

[49]   Sparks, 1984, 142.

[50]   Schürer, 1909, 3.396 cautiously observes that the decision as to Jewish provenance "aus dem vorliegenden Material läßt sich nicht mit einiger Sicherheit, nicht einmal mit Wahrscheinlichkeit vollziehen."

[51]   Kaufmann, 1932, 1.789.

a. Satan as fallen angel: *1 Enoch* 6f.; *Apocalypse of Abraham* 14; *b. Yoma* 67b; *Deuteronomy Rabba* 2.11 towards end; *Yalqut* to Gen 6.2; *Pirqe de Rabbi Eliezer* 27;
b. Satan's envy of humans: *b. Sanhedrin* 38b; *Genesis Rabba* 17.5
c. Adam's superiority to angels, *ibid.*
c. Angel prays for Adam: *Genesis Rabba* 8.9;
e. Serpent as Satan's instrument: *Pirqe de Rabbi Eliezer* 13;
f. Serpent has human hands (*Apocalypse of Moses* 26): cf. *Genesis Rabba* 19.1, 20.11, etc.
g. The forbidden tree is a fig (*Apocalypse of Moses* 21-22); R. Nehemiah in *b. Berakot* 40a; *b. Sanhedrin* 70b; *Genesis Rabba* 15.7
h. Poison in fruit (*Apocalypse of Moses* 19): cf. *3 Baruch* 47, *Apocalypse of Abraham* 13.
i. Mourning for seven days, and some other minor traditions.[52]

To these features, Ginzberg adds that in *Abot de Rabbi Nathan* 1.6 Eve called Adam "Lord" which is explained by the Adam book.[53] Schürer-Vermes-Millar, while displaying a more sophisticated list of Jewish features, have not made the case for the uniquely Jewish character of these features.[54]

More general considerations for its Jewish provenance had been adduced already by Fuchs. He notes, *inter alia*, that the story has the form of a Haggada and uses biblical text in midrashic fashion (this we judge doubtful), and that details of its cosmology and anthropology are such as might be found in a writing of Jewish origin.[55]

---

[52]   Kaufmann, 1932, 790-91.

[53]   Ginzberg, 1901, 1. 179-180.

[54]   Schürer-Vermes-Millar, 1978, 3.2, 758-759.

[55]   Fuchs, 1900, 510-11. Wells claims that the book is purely Jewish in origin and employs similar arguments to Fuchs' but also notes absence "even of Christian higher moral teaching" (p.127): see *ibid* 126-127. Above, the arguments were noted that the book is "pre-Rabbinic" which seem to conflict with this view. Bamberger, 1962, 45 also claims that the books "are well within the traditions of the Palestinian Haggada."

As to its more specific provenance, Wells holds that the authors were Jewish Hellenists, this view being imposed in his mind by the evidence for Greek originals of all versions on the one hand and evidence for Hebrew phrases on the other.[56] A similar view is espoused by Denis, although his argumentation is less naïve.[57] Bertrand proposes that *Apocalypse of Moses* originated probably in Egypt, among Egyptian Jewry. He adduces a number of motifs which most likely come from such a Jewish Hellenistic context: the chariot with psychopompic eagles that take up Adam's body; lake Acheron; the funeral instructions for Adam which are inspired by the Illiad; and the triangular seal on the protoplasts' tomb.[58] Denis, in the second edition of his *Introduction*, adds that perhaps also the catharsis by fire is Greek, quoting *Apocalypse of Moses* 37:3. Bertrand argues, furthermore, that the form of the pericopes with these Hellenistic themes is more primitive in the *Apocalypse of Moses* than the parallel material in Latin *Vita Adam et Evae*.[59]

Kaufmann argued for the origin of the Adam book in "Jewish mystical, perhaps even Essene" circles. He stressed:

a. Ascetic separation of male and female (*Apocalypse of Moses* 15) and ascetic attitude to sex (*Apocalypse of Moses* 25);
b. prominence of angels and oath by angel (*Apocalypse of Moses* 19, 32);
c. mystical setting of male to northeast and female to southwest (Latin *Vita Adam et Evae* 18f., *Apocalypse of Moses* 15);
d. view of animal sacrifices (*Apocalypse of Moses* 29, 33-36).[60]

While his understanding of what was "Jewish mystical, perhaps even Essene" was the product of his own era, there is no doubt that this list of

---

[56]   Wells, 1913, 126-127.

[57]   Denis, 1970, 6. He talks of Christian interpolations, e.g. 42.8, cf. Luke 23:46; 43:5, perhaps 36:3.

[58]   Bertrand, 1987a, 32-35.

[59]   Bertrand, 1987a, 35-36.

[60]   Kaufmann, 1932, 792.

characteristics is one that must be taken into account in any future studies of the context of the Adam literature.

Once more, Sparks takes a cautious position. He observes that "Jewish legends connected with Adam and Eve and their children abound. ... Yet there is no direct evidence for the existence of any pre-Christian written collection of these legends in either Hebrew or Aramaic." Consequently he concludes that *Apocalypse of Moses* contains nothing necessarily Christian, but that it is not therefore necessarily Jewish.[61]

4. Literary Interrelationships

General Considerations

In the preceding discussion, we have referred repeatedly to questions of literary interrelationships that must be resolved if the study of the primary Adam writings is to advance. The most basic of these issues, which to date have barely been touched by serious research, can be formulated as follows:

a. Do all the extant primary Adam writings, i.e. Latin *Vita Adam et Evae,* Slavonic *Vita Adam et Evae,* the Armenian *Penitence of Adam,* the Georgian *Life of Adam,* and the Coptic Adam book go back to Greek originals? As a correlative question, are any parts of these six forms of the work, or any of the particular tendencies or concerns to be discerned in them, products of the Christian traditions within which they were transmitted, not deriving from the Greek originals? Except for the possibility of Bogomil influence in the case of the Slavonic version, which seems to be a red herring, this problem has scarcely been broached.

b. How is the relationship between these five versions to be described? Can this relationship be formulated as that of five different reworkings of an original? If so, were the reworkings made from a single Greek translation of a putative Semitic original or were there a number of dif-

---

61   Sparks, 1984, 142. Battifol, 1895, 1. 764-765 claims that the book is Christian and of the fifth century. Much of the pre-Christian, Jewish material on Adam and Eve is gathered by Levison, 1988.

ferent Greek translations of this Semitic original? Alternatively, if the original was in Greek, what relationship do the extant works bear to it?

In answering these fundamental questions, the following methodological principles should be considered:

a. The various versions must be studied first of all in their own terms and their particular concerns and interests should be isolated by a process of comparison, without any preconceptions about which version is most primitive and which derivatory. The differences so discerned must then be considered first in the context of the particular Christian tradition in which the work was transmitted. They may be explicable on these grounds, or they may not. The answer to this question is central for any further investigation.[62]

b. The study of parallel texts in the Hebrew Bible, in the Gospels in the New Testament, and in Rabbinic and early Jewish mystical literature has brought about a great refinement of scholarly tools which might be applied to the parallel Adam writings. Which pericopes are shared and which not; can particular formulations be argued to be derivatory and others more original, and the like, are questions that must be posed, and might be answered, using methods developed in the study of parallel traditions in other, analogous fields of literature. A new Synopsis of the primary Adam books is under preparation and will prove a helpful tool in this task.[63]

c. It may be necessary to entertain other paradigms of authorship and transmission than simply original and derivative forms. The implications of synoptic studies of the Gospels on the one hand and of the Hechaloth literature on the other should teach us both caution and sensitivity to these possibilities.

---

[62]   This methodological issue is investigated by an unpublished, but widely circulated paper by R.A. Kraft, entitled: "The Pseudepigrapha in Christianity." Above, in Chapter 2, the characterization of *Apocalypse of Moses* and of Latin *Vita Adam et Evae* by Levison in his book *Portraits of Adam* is discussed. He has advanced more than his predecessors in treating these two versions in their own right, but has not taken the question of the Christian transmission into account.

[63]   It is being edited by G.A. Anderson and M.E. Stone in collaboration with W. Lechner-Schmidt.

An example of the unclarity of the present results of the scholarly discussion of this issue is the following quotation from the generally sound introduction by M.D. Johnson. Talking of the Latin *Vita Adam et Evae* he says:

> Whether the Latin is derived solely from a Greek version, partly from a Greek and partly from a Hebrew, or entirely from a Hebrew text cannot be determined conclusively.[64]

Yet the determination of these questions must lie at the basis of almost everything else that is to be said or done about the Adam books. Johnson goes on, in discussion of *Apocalypse of Moses*, to note that this Greek work bears signs of composite origins: God twice appears to announce punishment for sin (chapters 8 and 22) and twice to attend to death of Adam (chapters 33 and 38). Again *aporia* overwhelms him: "Several possibilities remain: The Latin author was ignorant of the Greek; he chose not to reproduce the story of Eve; or he had before him a form of the Greek text that is earlier than what is reflected in the extant manuscripts. The latter possibility seems most adequate."[65]

Proposed Views of the Literary Relationships

Fuchs, and Wells in his footsteps, made a careful attempt to deal in some detail with main differences of content between the three versions available to him. Fuchs argued that *Apocalypse of Moses* did not know the Latin *Vita Adam et Evae* but that Latin *Vita Adam et Evae* knew *Apocalypse of Moses*. Moreover, many of the plusses of Slavonic *Vita Adam et Evae* and of Latin *Vita Adam et Evae* are made up of indubitably Jewish material known in midrashim. Therefore, he concludes, the authors of these works knew both *Apocalypse of Moses* and also other Jewish sources, and Slavonic *Vita Adam et Evae* may have known the Greek original of Latin *Vita Adam et Evae*.[66] Wells regards Latin, Armenian and Slavonic as ancient versions of *Apocalypse of Moses*. He also, happily, refers to the later Christian works, our secondary Adam

---

[64]   Johnson, 1985, 251.

[65]   Johnson, 1985, 250.

[66]   Fuchs, 1900, 508-09. He is followed closely by Wells, 1913, 127-129.

writings, as "versions of the Adam books." However, he also admits the possibility that certain parts of the special material of both the Greek and the Latin works may be derived from independent ancient sources.[67]

These two scholars, and particularly Fuchs, have made the closest studies so far of the textual interrelationship of the Greek, Latin and Slavonic books. Their work should be reviewed carefully in light of the broader knowledge we now have of the Adam books and of the refined tools of analysis now at our disposal. Levison also prepared a table of the contents of the Greek and Latin books, emphasizing the unique material of each, as well as the synoptic or shared material.[68] He nowhere explains why, writing in 1988, he has ignored the existence of the Armenian and Georgian versions, of which he is apparently unconscious, citing neither Mahé nor Stone in his bibliography. This is regrettable, since a good deal of what he has to say about the meaning and purpose of *Apocalypse of Moses* and of Latin *Vita Adam et Evae* is vitiated by this lack. Yet his analysis remains a significant one indeed.

Levison is much concerned to prove the range and variety of the Adam literature and that this diversity was its character from ancient times. He quotes with approbation the remark of S.E. Robinson that, "we are dealing with a whole cycle of Adam literature originating in the intertestamental period and continuing to expand well into Christian times."[69] Levison regards this view as controverting the idea of a Semitic *Vorlage* of the primary Adam books, but we fail to see the necessary connection. Some or all of this range and variety of literature may have had a Semitic *Vorlage*, and there still might have been a single work which formed the basis of the surviving primary Adam writings. The dating declared by Robinson and accepted implicitly by Levison remains sheer speculation.

At the broad literary level, Nickelsburg has done some comparative analysis of the Greek and Latin works. He notes that the textual

---

[67]   Wells, 1913, 123-24.

[68]   Levison, 1988, 164.

[69]   Levison, 1988, 28 quoting Robinson, 1982, 16.

overlap of Latin and Greek is about one half. He suggests (1) that Latin *Vita Adam et Evae* 1-22 may be viewed as an elaborate form of *Apocalypse of Moses* 29:3-7; (2) that Adam's revelation to Seth in Latin *Vita Adam et Evae* 25-29 is a transformation the last part of Eve's narrative in *Apocalypse of Moses* 15-30; and (3) that Adam's second revelation to Seth (Latin *Vita Adam et Evae* 29:2-10) may be drawn from an earlier Adam testament. He has also stressed, for example, the implications of the testamentary character of Eve's narrative (*Apocalypse of Moses* 15-29). About *Apocalypse of Moses* he concludes: "Either *Apoc. Mos.* is an expansion of Genesis 3-4, influenced by elements of the testament form, or it is a redacted version of a testament of Adam, revised in line with the redactor's theological concerns."[70] Nickelsburg has dealt in some detail with the bearing of the broader literary structural questions upon the interrelationship of the primary Adam works (all of which he knew, except for the Georgian and Coptic). He concluded: "the *Apocalypse of Moses* is a more original form of the work. The *Vita* is an expansion of the earlier work — although it may contain some original elements that have dropped out of the *Apocalypse* and some original wording now revised in the *Apocalypse*. The Slavonic and Armenian versions are related and intermediate steps in the recensional process."[71] This is one of the few pieces of research that attempt to broach such issues and is praiseworthy for that. Its results will have to be carefully considered in future work on the topic, although in our view much more detailed analysis will be needed before final conclusions of this magnitude are drawn.

Bertrand carried out a study of the burial traditions and attitudes to the culpability of Adam and Eve.[72] In this research, he at-

---

[70]   Nickelsburg, 1981, 519. Nickelsburg set forth his views in a more succinct fashion in Nickelsburg, 1984, 110-18. The testamentary character of *Apocalypse of Moses* had already been pointed out by Battifol, 1895, 765.

[71]   Nickelsburg, 1984, 116.

[72]   On this topic see Charlesworth, 1979, 77-81. The different views he presents are: (a) that Adam is absolved (*Adam and Eve* 18:1, *2 Enoch* 31); (b) that the woman is responsible (Sirach); (c) both are culpable (*1 Enoch* 98:4f. *Liber Antiquitatum Biblicarum* 13:8 [but still chiefly Eve]); (d) Adam alone is mentioned (4 Ezra, *2 Apocalypse of Baruch* [54:19]). See also *Apocalypse of Sedrach* 5. A.B. Kolenkow, 1977, 1-11, recognizes the vari-

tempted to use the complexes of ideas and presuppositions exhibited by these burial traditions, combined with literary critical criteria, to elucidate certain issues of primacy between the Greek and Latin works. Again, in our view, much is to be learned from Bertrand's method, but we are forced to dissent from his very high evaluation of the Greek text of *Apocalypse of Moses.* The problems engendered by this are evident in his own work, from the fact that he had to make substantial ameliorations of the Greek text in order to "recover" its primitive form.[73] Using this method, however, Bertrand "clarified" the burial traditions which, not very remarkably, now fitted his theory. Moreover, the original glorification of Adam, we are told, was often reduced by the Christian tradents of the book under the influence of the idea of Christ as the true Adam.[74] There is, of course, little evidence in the book for this original glorification of Adam beyond Bertrand's reconstruction.

These are examples of the approaches by which some scholars have tried to clarify the relationships between the texts.[75] The number of patterns of relationship proposed is not excessive. We summarize them as follows:

a. *There was an original (Hebrew or Aramaic) book from which the primary Adam writings derive:* For example, Kaufmann proposes that there was an original Adam book, ancestor of the three "primary Adam

---

ety of the burial traditions in *Apocalypse of Moses* and in Latin *Vita Adam et Evae* and makes the strange observation: "The alternate versions of what happens to Adam immediately after death ... show how two possible alternative presentations of a situation may be used to emphasize an author's own philosophy" (p. 4). It is difficult to conceive what this statement implies about her view of the genesis of the primary Adam writings and the relationship between them. Kolenkow has not, it seems to us, thought out what her statement implies in terms of literary history.

73   Bertrand, 1985, 112-115. An attempt to put these burial traditions into the context of ancient burial practice is made by Cousin, 1974, 384-386.

74   Bertrand, 1985, 116-118. The glorification of Adam is also dealt with in some detail by Bianchi, 1969, 9-11. See further Levison, 1988, *passim.*

75   Frey, 1928, 1. cols. 103-105 gives a fine survey of scholarly opinion on the provenance, character and interrelationship of the *Apocalypse of Moses* and Latin *Vita Adam et Evae* up to his day. He himself supports the idea of a Jewish origin, a date in the first century C.E., and a Hebrew original.

books" known to him. He suggests that this was a Jewish work, written in Hebrew. Eissfeldt proposed a similar view for the "basic material" of Latin *Vita Adam et Evae* and *Apocalypse of Moses*.[76] Torrey also claimed that the different versions go back to a single Greek translation made from a Jewish, Aramaic archetype and that variation between them is due to the "the reproduction from memory which would be normal in such folklore as this".[77] According to Kaufmann, this underlying writing contained the following material (in fact, a conflation of all the plusses of both the Latin and the Greek works):

1. The Penitence (Latin *Vita Adam et Evae* only).
2. Satan's reason for enmity (Latin *Vita Adam et Evae* only).
3. Birth of Adam's children (*Apocalypse of Moses* and Latin *Vita Adam et Evae*).
4. Adam's story of his heavenly vision (Latin *Vita Adam et Evae*).
5. Adam's illness and Seth and Eve's quest (Latin *Vita Adam et Evae* and *Apocalypse of Moses*).
6. Eve's story of her sin (*Apocalypse of Moses*).
7. Adam's death and the mourning (Latin *Vita Adam et Evae* and *Apocalypse of Moses*).[78]

An even more radical form of this notion is the opinion of Götze, quoted with approbation by Frey, that there existed a "*Livre d'Adam* primitif, écrit en hébreu ou en araméen, qui est à base des *Jubilés*, de la *Vita* et de l'*Apocalypse de Moïse*, de l'haggade juive des *Ps.-Clémentines* et de toute la littérature apocryphe adamique chrétienne, qui est antérieur à l'ère chrétienne."[79] This broad theory at-

---

[76]   Eissfeldt, 1965, 636.

[77]   Torrey, 1945, 131-133; the quotation is from p. 132.

[78]   Kaufmann, 1932. Ginzberg, 1901 suggests a basically similar content but arranges it in chronological order. Hartom suggests that the Latin and Greek books are reworkings done in the early Christian centuries, of a Hebrew work from the end of the Second Temple period which is perhaps referred to in *b Baba Meṣia* 85b; *Genesis Rabba* 24.2f., *Leviticus Rabba* 15.1, *Midrash Qohelet* on 1.6 (Hartom, 1965, 9-10). On these Rabbinic sources, see Chapter 3 below.

[79]   Frey, 1928, 115. This view is attacked energetically by Levison, 1988, 28.

tempts to account not merely for the common material of our primary Adam writings, but also for what have been identified as clearly Jewish elements in such works as *Cave of Treasures* and *Conflict of Adam and Eve with Satan.* It cannot be regarded as proven, but it certainly highlights broader issues in the study of the Adam literature that await renewed and even more thorough research.

b. *The Greek* Apocalypse of Moses *is original, but it was composed on the basis of Jewish traditions:* Sparks, for example, does not clarify completely his view of the Greek *Apocalypse of Moses.* However, he says that Latin *Vita Adam et Evae* "is best explained as the translation either of a later recension of the 'Apocalypse', or, possibly but less probably, of one of the sources behind the 'Apocalypse'."[80] Thus he seems to allow some sources (Greek? or Hebrew?) behind *Apocalypse of Moses* which was composed in Greek.[81] A similar position is taken by Bertrand, who talks of a Judaeo-Greek style and underlying Hebrew or Aramaic Jewish Adam traditions, but avoids claiming the existence of a Hebrew or Aramaic original.[82] Schürer-Vermes-Millar argue that the Greek *Apocalypse of Moses* is the most original, and that it was known to the author of the Latin *Vita Adam et Evae.* Yet they also argue that the Greek work is Jewish with Christian additions, and to substantiate that, they cite, *inter alia*, so-called Jewish traditions to be found only in the Latin *Vita Adam et Evae.*[83] Their position on the original language does not vary greatly from that of Bertrand.

c. *The Greek, substantially the present form of the* Apocalypse of Moses, *is original:* Although Bertrand claims that each of the primary Adam writings derives from a Greek original, not necessarily in the form now preserved as *Apocalypse of Moses*, nonetheless, he maintains, the surviving Greek *Apocalypse of Moses* is most primary both upon literary and on doctrinal grounds. He proclaims that to prove this it suffices

---

80   Sparks, 1984, 143.

81   It is unclear whether written or oral sources are intended by Sparks, though it seems that Bertrand's "traditons" may well have been oral.

82   Bertrand, 1987a, 26-27.

83   Schürer-Vermes-Millar, 1987, 758.

to show priority of Greek over Latin since this is, *a priori*, the only relationship that might be reversed, "à ne considérer que la date probablement très ancienne des deux versions."[84] The primacy of the Greek *Apocalypse of Moses* among the surviving versions is also maintained by Kahana.[85] Similarly, Denis claims that Greek is probably oldest recension, into which various legends have been inserted in the other versions. The Latin is reworked by abbreviation and insertion, but preserves some passages omitted by Greek.[86]

d. *The Georgian is the best Witness to the Adam Book:* The position taken by Mahé is that "Dans l'état actuel de notre documentation, c'est le géorgien, corrigé à l'aide de l'arménien confirmé par le grec ou le latin, qui permet de connaître le mieux la *Vie* apocryphe d'Adam et Eve."[87] This position is not far from that taken by the present writer in his publication of the Armenian *Penitence of Adam* that: (a) in a number of places examined, the Armenian *Penitence of Adam* preserves a text preferable to both Greek and Latin; (b) in other places, its unique readings are corroborated or supported by sources outside the Adam books; (c) the story line of the Armenian is probably primitive. I concluded "However, a definite conclusion ... should probably only be drawn after a careful study of the Georgian version in particular."[88] These remarks have not been taken into account by those studying the texts since then, nor have the arguments by which Mahé and I supported our claims been addressed.

---

84   Bertrand, 1987a, 24. On pp. 24-25 he discusses a series of texts designed to prove this. According to him, the book has two chief topics: (a) sort of expanded form of Gen 2-4; (b) burial of protoplasts: so Bertrand, 1985, 109-110. He goes into this in greater detail in 1987a, 23-24. On p. 24 he claims that the present writer maintains the primacy of the Greek vis à vis the Armenian *Penitence of Adam*. This is not our view, however, and see comments in our review of his book in Stone, 1990.

85   Kahana, 1956, 1.[2]-[3].

86   Denis, 1970, 6-7. Concerning Latin *Vita Adam et Evae* he proposes that although 29.2-7 is old, it is an insertion into the work, as is the vision of Adam which precedes (25-29). On this he quotes Nagel.

87   Mahé, 1983, 65.

88   Stone, 1981a, x-xi.

e. *There existed an "Adam Cycle" of which* Apocalypse of Moses
formed a part: Denis also introduces another factor into the discussion.
He talks of an "Adam cycle" and says that *Apocalypse of Moses* "fait
partie d'un important cycle d'Adam. Il existe en entier en version ar-
ménienne, mais souvent remanié et christianisé."[89] The cycle also
largely exists, he claims, in Slavonic and he would apparently attribute
all the Christian Adam writings to this cycle.[90] If by "Adam Cycle"
Denis denotes an actual corpus of writings that existed as a whole in antiquity, of which we have a surviving form in Armenian, then his assertion will require further demonstration.[91] Bertrand, in the introduction
to his text edition of the Greek *Apocalypse of Moses*, also seems unclear
as to the difference between a translation of an extant work, a different
version of the same underlying material, and secondary Adam books
which may draw inspiration from the "primary Adam writings" but must
be regarded as independent compositions. This unclarity comes out at
many points in his introduction. Thus he speaks of an Armenian *Life of
Adam and Eve* which exists in two recensions,[92] yet this is quite mis-
leading. In fact there is an Armenian translation of *Apocalypse of
Moses* which is a direct witness to the Greek, while the Armenian *Penitence of Adam* is a different primary Adam book, to be regarded at the
same level of transmission as the Latin, Slavonic and Georgian versions.

---

[89]   Denis, 1970, 7. By this Armenian Adam cycle, he surely meant those of
the Armenian secondary Adam books which he knew. On these, see
below, chap. 4, sect. 6. However, the works he knew are themselves very
diverse, and certainly do not form a single cycle in Armenian. Those additional Armenian Adam writings newly made known complicate the picture even more. In our opinion, the Armenian Adam books neither support nor controvert the view that there existed, in antiquity, a broad
"cycle d'Adam", and the question of the sources of the Armenian Adam
books has not yet been thoroughly researched, let alone resolved.

[90]   Denis, 1970, 8: his observations on each of them are incorporated above.

[91]   Bamberger, 1901 also seems to claim the existence of a Jewish Adam
cycle, including a number of primary and secondary Adam books, and
connected with the ספרא דאדם ראשון mentioned in Rabbinic literature (7-25;
see also Chapter 2, section 1 above). Bamberger would connect this literature with *Jubilees*.

[92]   Bertrand, 1987a, 18.

The Functioning of the Primary Adam Books in their Christian Context

Bertrand, in a pioneering section of the introduction to his Greek edition, has raised and attempted to respond to the issue we mentioned: the function of the *Apocalypse of Moses* in the Christian context in which it was copied and preserved. On the one hand, he discerns a series of Christian touches. On the other, he examines its function in the codices in which it was found: the context is one of apocryphal and homiletic works.[93] He also turns his mind to the question of the liturgical function of *Apocalypse of Moses* as well as its influence in Christian literature.[94]

5. Researches on Specific Topics

There have been a number of researches written on specific dimensions of the primary Adam books. It is clearly beyond our scope to present all of these, but certain paradigmatic studies may be mentioned.

E.C. Quinn carefully investigated the tradition of Eve's and Seth's journey to the Garden of Eden to seek healing for Adam.[95] This study, as well as paying attention to the roots of the story in the history-of-religions background, also traced its stupendous influence through medieval literature and art. Of course, even more could be done on the ramifications of this material in medieval literature. A.B. Kolenkow has also studied this story, relating it to shamanistic materials known from anthropological research. First, she stresses the role of Seth that emerges in this story as told in the Greek and Latin primary Adam writings. Next, she investigates the nature of Seth's otherworldly trip, his receipt of revelation, and the possible implications of the failure of his mission.[96]

---

93   Bertrand, 1987a, 61-63. This material had already been documented in great detail by Nagel, 1974.

94   Bertrand, 1987a, 63.

95   Quinn, 1962. See also the observations of Evans, 1968 on the literary development of these themes: see further Chapter 4, below.

96   Kolenkow, 1977, 1-11.

In a most interesting article, S. Lieberman showed how a story of
Lot's repentance and bringing three branches from the Garden of Eden,
which is related in the Greek *Palaea*, is connected with the story of the
quest of Seth.[97] He also adduced some forms of the Seth story in European languages, but opines that the form of the material in the Greek
and Latin primary Adam books contains nothing inherently Christian
and he reconstructs a Jewish form of it.[98]

In two articles, U. Bianchi broached a number of issues in the
conceptual background of the Adam writings (assuming a Jewish document behind the primary Adam books): the exaltation of Adam, the
view of woman, the idea of Adam's knowledge,[99] and the view of history
as a history of salvation, with which he sees the book(s) to be per-
meated.[100] He contrasts the views of the Adam books with those of Paul,
as well as with later Christian and gnostic conceptions. N. Forsyth argues
(unconvincingly) that the Adam and Eve traditions derive from the
Enoch ones. In particular, he claims that the figure of Seth derives from
Enoch; Satan (or the serpent) seduces Eve, which incident derives from
the story of the lust of the Watchers for the daughters of men in Enoch,
and so forth.[101]

Sharpe in a paper on "The Second Adam in the Apocalypse of
Moses" examined the idea of Adam's sin in the context of the Pauline
view of Adam and Christ. He argues that the sin was disobedience, and
that Adam's eating of the forbidden fruit resembled other human sins

---

[97] See Vassiliev, 1893, 218; Lieberman, 1972, 44-45. Another version of this
story is in the poem of Georgios Chumnos, see below Chapter 4, section
1. We may add that yet another form of this story is part of the foundation
legend of the Monastery of the Cross in Jerusalem: see V. Tzaferis, 1987,
8. In the sanctuary of the monastery's church hangs a series of paintings
depicting that story. See also the forms of this legend of Seth and the oil
extant in Armenian, which are mentioned below Chapter 4, section 3.

[98] Lieberman, 1972, 45-46.

[99] So Bianchi, 1969.

[100] This is the theme of his paper: U. Bianchi, 1971, 1-8.

[101] Forsyth, 1987, 228-242.

of disobedience. The immediate result of the sin was the loss of glory and of righteousness, but not of the εἰκών of God. After his death Adam is pardoned and taken to Paradise in the third heaven. In the future the holy people will be saved together with Adam. Sharpe attempts to draw a series of detailed parallels between *Apocalypse of Moses* and Pauline thought, aiming to demonstrate Paul's dependance upon first century B.C.E. Jewish thought, as presented in *Apocalypse of Moses*.[102]

In an article stimulated by the text of the Middle High German *Wiener Genesis* and the *Anegenge*, Murdoch discusses the idea of the wondrous or angelic garments of Adam and Eve. He traces the idea of these garments back in Jewish and Christian exegesis to earliest times. Of particular note to him is the expression *daz engliske gewate* found in *Wiener Genesis* (line 972) which he sees as perhaps originating from the expression "a little less than the angels" (Psalm 8:6).[103]

In a folklore orientated study, the same author discussed the motif of the waters that stood still.[104] In the Latin *Vita Adam et Evae* 8:2 the waters of the Jordan are said to stand while Adam prays in them (*statim omnia animantia venerunt et circumdederunt eum et aqua Jordanis stetit ab illa hora non agens cursum suum*). Murdoch traces this motif from Latin *Vita Adam et Evae* into *Saltair na Rann* and *Pennaid Adam* in old Irish. He further points out how, in various medieval versions, the *omnia animantia* of the Latin text are expanded into lists of created beings. In the Jewish material on the penitence of Adam, however, in *Pirqe de Rabbi Eliezer,* there is no mention of waters standing still.[105] This motif may come from folktales in which it is generally connected with birth of god, king or cult-hero. He further observes that in the Greek *Protoevangalium Jacobi* an analogous theme

---

102　Sharpe, 1973, 35-46. This matter is also dealt with at some length by Levison, 1988, passim.

103　Murdoch, 1967, 375-382. On the garments, compare also the material adduced in Chapter 4, section 3.

104　Murdoch, 1973, 37-51.

105　See Lévi, 1889.

exists, related to the birth of Christ and that this might have influenced the *Vita Adam et Evae* either at Greek or at Latin level.[106]

It appears therefore, that in spite of substantial advances made, particularly in the area of the publication of texts, a good deal remains to be done in the study of the primary Adam books. Our view is that the clarification of interrelationship among the versions is an extremely pressing need. Equally important is to understand how the various primary Adam books functioned in the Christian contexts in which they were transmitted and through that to be able to assess their extant forms.

The next two chapters will provide the reader with information on Adam literature beyond the primary Adam books. First, ancient evidence for the existence of further Adam writings will be presented, and then, in the fourth chapter a survey of the secondary Adam writings in a number of languages will be made.

---

[106] Murdoch, 1973, 41-49. In our view, the relationship between these elements of *Protoevangelium Jacobi* and the *Vita Adam et Evae* is not close enough for the argument made by Murdoch to be conclusive.

CHAPTER 3

TESTIMONIA AND REFERENCES TO ADAM BOOKS

1. Direct Ancient Testimonies

In this section we have assembled the chief references to the existence of an Adam book or books in ancient and Byzantine sources. These references are of varied character and weight, and do not necessarily all refer to the same document. They are additional to the manuscript evidence for whole or fragmentary works which is discussed in the preceding and following chapters. Such testimonia often have a history of their own, and they form part of the story of the Adam literature.

1. *Constitutiones Apostolorum* 6.16.3. This work, a book of church order attributed to the Apostles, is commonly dated to the fourth century.

> Καὶ ἐν τοῖς παλαιοῖς δέ τινες συνέγραψαν βιβλία ἀπόκρυφα Μωυσέως καὶ Ἐνὼχ καὶ Ἀδάμ, Ἡσαίου τε καὶ Δαυὶδ καὶ Ἡλίου καὶ τῶν τριῶν πατριαρχῶν, φθοροποιὰ καὶ τῆς ἀληθείας ἐχθρά·

> And in the ancient times, certain persons composed apocrypha of Moses and Enoch and Adam, of Isaiah and David and Elijah and of the three patriarchs, which are pernicious and inimical to the truth.

2. The Byzantine *List of Sixty Books,* falsely attributed to Anastasius Sinaïta, and apparently dating to the sixth century, has "Adam" at the head of the list of works outside the sixty books of scripture.[1]

3. The Slavonic list of Pseudo-Anastasius.[2] This is a translation of the *List of Sixty Books.*

4. Gelasian Decree: this list is traditionally attributed to Pope Gelasius (492-496), but was actually written somewhat later, probably in the sixth century. It

---

[1]   Denis, 1970, xii.

[2]   Lüdtke, 1911, 230-235, cf. Denis, 1970, xii, xiv. Adam is first in all the six forms of the list as published by Lüdtke.

75

is a list of books and their status. Two lines mention works connected with Adam. The title "Leptogenesis" or "Little Genesis" which is found in line 4.7 usually refers to the *Book of Jubilees*. Its use here is problematic and has raised a considerable amount of speculation.

> 6.2 *Liber qui appelatur paenitentia Adae, apocryphus*[3]
> 4.7 *Liber de filiabus Adæ Leptogeneseos.*[4]

> 6.2 Book which is called *Penitence of Adam*, apocryphal.
> 4.7 Book concerning the daughters of Adam, of *Leptogenesis*.

5. Suda *s.v.* Αδαμ· The *Suda* is an encyclopedic work composed about 1000 C.E. and produced in the Byzantine Empire. It often preserves ancient traditions.

> τούτου προφητεῖαι, ἱερουργίαι καὶ καθαρμοὶ καὶ νόμοι γραπτοί τε καὶ ἄγραφοι. Τούτου πάντα εὑρήματα, καὶ διδάγματα, καὶ ὅσα τὸν βίον ἀναγκαῖαι χρεῖαί τε καὶ δίαιται.

> Of this one (i.e. Adam) there are prophecies, sacrifices and purifications and both written and unwritten laws. His are all discoveries and teachings and all necessary requirements and regiments for life.

6. Iosephi *Hypomnesticon*, cap. xv. The *Hypomnesticon* is attributed to a certain Josephus, a Christian, distinguished from Josephus Flavius the Jewish historian. The *Hypomnesticon* may have been written during the Byzantine period. It is a collection of information about biblical topics, arranged as its title would suggest, in list or mnemonic form. It has been little studied.

> Τίνες δὲ γεγόνασιν ἄλλοι προφῆται οἱ μὴ ἐν γράμμασιν αὐτῶν καταλείψαντες τὰς προφητείας;
> α, Ἀδαμ. β, Νῶε κ.τ.λ.

> There were certain other prophets who did not leave behind their prophecies in writing:

> 1. Adam; 2. Noah, etc.

---

[3]   von Dobschütz, 1912, line 297.

[4]   See von Dobschütz, 1912, line 285. This work is discussed in some detail by Frey, 1928, 153-154.

7. Armenian List of Mexit'ar Ayrivanec'i, in the list of Apocrypha. This is a list of biblical and apocryphal books prepared by the learned thirteenth-century Armenian cleric. His list of apocryphal books is of particular interest and probably goes back to a Greek original.

Գիրք որ ունին Հրեայքն ի ծածուկ այսորիկ են.
Ադամայ. են

These are the books which the Jews have in secret,
Of Adam, etc.[5]

8. Samuel of Ani was an Armenian historian of the thirteenth century. In his *Chronicle* he included in a list of books introduced into Armenia by Nestorian missionaries in 590 C.E. Among them, an Adam book is mentioned, but its exact title is unclear. According to Erevan Matenadaran Ms 1869 (1585-1589 C.E.), it was called *Ադամայ Կտակն* "Testament of Adam," while in the Vałašapat edition of the *Chronicle* published in 1893 we read *Ադամայ Ապաշխարութիւն* "Penitence of Adam." Both titles have support elsewhere in traditions about Adam books or as titles of existing Adam works.[6] In addition to this explicit reference either to a *Penitence* or a *Testament of Adam*, in line 8 of the list, the Armenian transliteration of Greek Διαθήκη is to be found. We do not consider this necessarily to be a reference to a *Testament of Adam*.[7]

9. Anastasius Sinaïta, *On the Hexaemeron*, 7.895 (*PG* 89.967) refers to a *Testament of the Protoplasts*. Anastasius lived in St. Catherine's monastery in the Sinai in the middle of the seventh century. The tradition related in this text is found already in *Jubilees* 3:9.

> Unde Hebræi ex libro qui non est redactus in Canonem, qui quidem dicitur Testamentum protoplastorum, dicunt quadragesima die ingressum esse Adam in paradisum.

---

[5]   Stone, 1976, 290.

[6]   See the text of Samuel's list in Anasyan, 1959, 1.xxxix and the discussion in Stone, 1982, 44.

[7]   See Stone, 1981a, *Translation*, ix.

Whence the Hebrews, from a book which is not included in the Canon, which indeed is said to be a *Testament of the Protoplasts*, say that on the fortieth day Adam entered Paradise.

10. The *Chronicle* of the ninth-century Byzantine court official George the Syncellus mentions βίος Ἀδάμ *Life of Adam*.[8] This work probably served as a source for the Syncellus as well as for George Cedrenus, both of whom drew upon the earlier chronographic traditions.[9]

11. The Syriac apocryphon *Transitus Mariae* preserves a tradition about Adam's testament which was eventually brought to Bethlehem by the Magi.[10] It does not seem likely that this actually reflects knowledge of a specific document.

12. Testimony to the existence of *Apocalypse of Adam* may be found in the margin of the Constantinople Ms (now Jerusalem, Greek Patriarchate 49) of Barnabas to 2:10 ψαλμ. Ν´ καὶ ἐν ἀποκαλύψει Ἀδάμ (fol. 39v). This marginal note implies that the citation given in the second century document, the *Epistle of Barnabas*, was drawn from a combination of Psalm 50 and an *Apocalypse of Adam*. This citation is certainly not to be found in the *Apocalypse of Adam* known from Nag Hammadi.

13. Denis observes that the Adam book is listed third in *Constitutiones Apostolorum* and first in the *List of Sixty Books*, in the list of Mexit'ar Ayrivanec'i and in all the Slavonic recensions of the lists of apocryphal books.[11] It is hard to know what significance might inhere in this. The point is made

---

[8]   Dindorf, 1829, 7-8; Mosshammer, 1984, 4-5.

[9]   See Schürer, 1909, 3.397. The question of Syncellus' sources is discussed by Gelzer, rpr. 1967, 261, 246-268. He considers that Syncellus knows the *Life of Adam* from fifth century Alexandrian sources. Adler, 1989, 84-86 argues for a post-fourth century date for the chronographers in the *Life of Adam*.

[10]   Robinson, 1982, 12. He gives a fuller translation and references to further literature on pp. 149-150. This work was translated from Syriac in the last century by Wright, 1865, 24-25.

[11]   Denis, 1970, 3.

by Bertrand that none of these testimonia can be taken unambiguously to refer to *Apocalypse of Moses.*[12]

14. The ספרא דאדם ראשון or ספרו של אדם הראשון, that is "The Book of the Protoplast Adam," which is mentioned in Rabbinic sources such as *b. Baba Meṣia* 85b-86a; *b. Sanhedrin* 38b; *Genesis Rabba.* 24.2 has nothing to do with Adam, but is a heavenly book of genealogies, cf. *1 Enoch* 81.1-2, 93.2, 103.2, 106.19, cf. also *b. Aboda Zara* 5a.[13] Kahana regards this as evidence for early Adam speculations.[14]

15. In the Samaritan work which J. Bowman entitles *The Malef,* of which he published a translation from a very late manuscript, the following is to be found, concerning the rod which Adam was believed to have taken with him on his expulsion from Eden:

> upon it was written the true (calendar) reckoning and the book of the wars and the book of the signs, and the book of astronomy. ... The three books were preserved until the coming of the apostle and some (parts) of them were with Laban and some with Balaam; but from the time of the coming of the Law they were defective until finally they departed from the world.[15]

16. Eutychius of Alexandria in his *Chronicle* quotes Adam traditions that know of a testamentary scene, of a cave like the Cave of Treasures, and of the

---

[12]   Bertrand, 1987a, 29.

[13]   Compare also Fabricius, 1713, 1.10-11. Robinson, 1982, 5-6 also cites the texts from *Genesis Rabba* and *b. Aboda Zara* as referring to some sort of *Book of Adam,* perhaps even a heavenly one, but not necessarily "a Book of Adam extant in Jewish circles in intertestamental times" (p. 6).

[14]   Kahana, 1956, 1.[1]. Schürer, 1909, 3.396 argues vigorously against the actual existence of this book which he regards as existing "nur in der Phantasie der Rabbinen." He also cites *Exodus Rabba* 40. The work is discussed by Bamberger, 1901. Schürer-Vermes-Millar, 1987, 3.2, 757n re-evaluate the evidence once more.

[15]   Bowman, 1981-82, 10.

date of Adam's death. These do not necessarily refer, however, to any specific ancient Adam writing.[16]

17. The Cologne Mani codex 48:15-50:7 includes material attributed to an Adam apocalypse. This material is unlike that found in any of the known Adam texts.[17]

48,16 [οὔτ]ῳ πρῶτο[ς] ὁ Αδαμ Ι [...... .].ωτ[..] εἶπεν [ἐν τῆι ἀποκαλύψει] αὐτοῦ·

. . .

49 '. . . λαμ]Ι ¹πρῦ προσώπου σου ὃν ἐΙγὼ οὐ γινώσκω.' τότε Ι ἔφη αὐτῶι· 'ἐγώ εἰμι ΒάλΙσαμος ὁ μέγιστος ἄγγειλος τοῦ φῶτος· ὅθεν δεΙξάμενος γράψον ταῦτα Ι ἅπερ σου ἀποκαλύπτω ἐν Ι ⁸ χάρτηι καθαρωτάτι καὶ Ι μὴ φθειρομέμωι καὶ σῆΙτα μὴ ἐπιδεχομέωι, χωΙρὶς καὶ ἄλλων πλείστων Ι ¹² ὧν αὐτῶι ἀπεκάλυψεν Ι ἐν τῆι ὀπτασίαι. μεγίστη Ι γὰρ ἦν ἡ περὶ αὐτὸν δόξα. Ι ἐθεώρησεν δὲ κα[ὶ τοὺς] Ι ¹⁶ ἀγγέλους κα[ὶ ἀρχιστρα]Ιτηγοὺ[ς καὶ δυνάμεις Ι μεγί[στας . . .

50,1 . . . ὁ Αδαμ καὶ γέγονεν Ι ὑπέρτερος παρὰ πάσας Ι τὰς δυνάμεις καὶ τοὺς Ι ⁴ ἀγγέλους τῆς κτίσεως. Ι πολλὰ δὲ καὶ ἄλλα τούτοις Ι παραπλήσια ὑπάρχει ἐν ταῖς γραφαῖς αὐτοῦ.Ι

---

16   The material is cited by von Nordheim, 1980, 176 from Migne, *PG* 111. col. 911. We reproduce the text here, for interest's sake:

Adamus, antea, appropinquante iam morte ipsius, convocatis filio suo Setho, Sethique Enosho, Enoshi Kainano, et Kainani Mahlaliele, praecepit, dicens ipsis: Sit hoc mandatum omnibus filiis vestris. Ubi mortuus fuero, corpus meum myrrha, thure et cassia conditum reponite in spelunca Alcanuz: et quicunque fuerit e filiis vestris eo tempore cum e confiniis paradisi abeundum vobis sit, corpus meum secum sublatum ponat in medio terrae, quoniam inde futura est salus mea, et salus omnium filiorum meorum.

Totum autem vitae Adami spatium erat nongentorum triginta annorum, ac mortuus est die Veneris, luna decima quarta, sexto Nisan (qui est Barmudah) hora nonadiei Veneris; qua enim fora e paradiso pulsus est. Mortuum ergo Adamum pollinxit, iuxta ipsius mandatum, filius eius Seth, corpusque eius ad fastigium montis sublatum inspelunca Alcanuz sepelivit: ipsumque centum quadraginta dies planxerunt.

17   See Henrichs-Koenen, 1975, 48-51. This fragment is discussed in some detail by Morard, 1985, 8-9.

48,16 [Thu]s said the first Adam ... said [in] his [apocalypse].

. . .

49 '. . . *before*] your [sh]ining countenance, which I do not know.' Then he said to him, 'I am Balsamos, the greatest angel of light. Thence, having received these things which I reveal to you, write them on purest and uncorrupted parchment, untouched by worms,' apart from many other things which he revealed to him in the vision. For the glory surrounding him was very great. He saw als[o the] angels an[d archistrateg[s and] very great [powers ...

50,1 . . . Adam also became higher than all the powers and the angels of creation. There are may other things like these in his writings.

18. There are some references to Gnostic or heretical Adam writings, see chapter 4, Appendix, below.

2. Traditions Assembled by J. Fabricius

The first significant collection of Old Testament pseudepigrapha, whole and fragmentary, was made in the eighteenth century by the Swiss Protestant scholar J. Fabricius.[18] Fabricius, a man of encyclopedic learning, assembled an unparalleled range of traditions relating to Adam, drawn from ancient and medieval sources alike. Quite a large part of these traditions gathered by Fabricius have never been taken up again by scholars or only rarely so, and it may be useful if we provide a conspectus of the material in Fabricius' collection, making no claims about the antiquity or authenticity of any specific item in this catalogue.[19] The chief ones concern:

a.   Adam's invention of Hebrew letters (1.1-2; 2.1-4).
b.   Adam's giving names to living beings (1.2-4; 2.4-5).
c.   Adam instructed by angels (1.4-5).

---

18   Much data on the early history of collections of pseudepigrapha may be found in Migne, 1856-58, 1.xxxiv-xxxviii.

19   Fabricius' work was published in two volumes. The first is Fabricius, 1713. The material on Adam is to be found there on pages 1-95. The second volume of the work is Fabricius, 1723. It contains supplements to the material published in the earlier, first volume and also the full text of the *Hypomnesticum* of Josephus. The citations below refer first to the relevant pages of volume 1 and then to the relevant pages of volume 2.

d.   Adam as "apostolus lunae" (1.5-6) - odd material.
e.   Adam, Prophet (1.6-7; 2.7-8).
f.   Adam Prometheus (1.7-9).
g.   Adam's Wondrous Powers (1.10; 2.11-12).
h.   Book of the Generations of Adam (1.10-11) - Rabbinic material.
i.   Apocalypses of Adam (1.11-12).
j.   Ὁ λεγόμενος Βίος Ἀδαμ (1.12-16) - the material from the Byzantine chronicler, Syncellus, discussed below, Chapter 4, section 1.
k.   Penitence of Adam (1.16-21) - Syncellus, Cedrenus, Raziel; (2.14-20). Isaac, Catholicus of Greater Armenia.
l.   Psalm 92 attributed to Adam (1.19-21) - Rabbinic.[20]
m.   Psalms related to Adam and Eve (1.21-26; 2.26-28).[21]
n.   Book of Raziel (1.26-27).
o.   Mandean Book of Adam (1.27-29); see below, Chapter 4, Appendix on Mandean literature.
p.   Sefer Yetzira (1.29-30).
q.-r. Moslem traditions (1.30-32; 2.30-36) — particularly relationship to Ceylon.
s.   Alchemical work (1.32-33).[22]
t.-u. Various Jewish traditions (1.33-35).
v.   Testament of Adam - traditions about (1.35-36).
w.   Medieval German Adam book (1.36-47).
x.-y. Varia 48-53.
z.   Concerning the Remains of Adam (1.53-94); - collection of various traditions; (2.37-39) - tomb.
aa.   Adam's wife, Lilith (2.5-7).
bb.   Adam's Philosophy (2.8-11).
cc.   Adam observed Sabbath in Paradise (2.13-14).
dd.   Place where Adam went in exile from Paradise (2.20-26).
ee.   Fruit (2.36-37).
ff.   Name of Adam (2.39-41, cf. 1.50).

---

[20]   See Migne, 1856-58, 2.41.

[21]   See Migne, 1856-58, 1.xli: he gives a French translation of this text on pp. 391-392.

[22]   See further Migne, 1856-58, 2.42 on this material.

gg.   Stature of Adam (2.41-42).

hh.   Epitaph of Adam (2.42-43).

CHAPTER 4

THE SECONDARY ADAM LITERATURE

The literature that is discussed in this chapter comprises in the first place numerous works that were written in antiquity about Adam and Eve and their progeny. These were chiefly Christian or (less often) Jewish or Gnostic compositions, and are in general influenced directly or indirectly by the primary Adam books. There are many of these works, and if, in addition, the medieval writings dealing with the protoplasts are brought into account, then the catalogue of secondary Adam writings becomes far too long for them to be dealt with fully here. In the present chapter the chief early books of this type are described. Certain later works are mentioned as well, without any attempt at exhaustiveness in range or bibliography. The richness of the development of the Adam traditions will thus be made very evident and their implications for many dimensions of European and Oriental literature and culture will emerge.[1]

1. Adam Writings in Greek

Certain of the works attributed to Adam by Greek sources have already been mentioned in the third chapter of the present book which dealt with ancient testimonia to the existence of Adam literature.[2] Because of

---

[1] Because our concery is first and foremost with documents dealing with Adam and Eve, we do not discuss thematic scholarly monographs on various aspects of the traditions about the protoplasts. There are not a few of these. Some were mentioned in note 1 to the Introductory remarks. Other significant works include: Anderson, 1989; Aptowitzer, 1922; Klijn, 1977; Niditch, 1983, 137-146; Stichel, 1971; Stone, 1981c. This list is by no means complete.

[2] Compare also Chapter 1, above. It should be observed that the exegesis of the Adam and Eve stories was a major topic in patristic writing. Furthermore, in artistic representations of Adam and Eve, often hints may survive of narrative incidents not preserved explicitly or only found infrequently in the ancient or early medieval Adamic apocrypha. For example, one such incident is Adam's naming of the animals, which was important

the fragmentary nature of the evidence, some overlapping of the present section with Chapter 3 is inevitable. The Greek primary and secondary Adam literature is curiously sparse and the chief evidence for it is fragmentary. The main works that have some claim to existence are the following.

1. *Apocalypse of Adam*: As noted above, the chief direct evidence for the existence of this work is a marginal notation in the manuscript of the *Epistle of Barnabas*. Other evidence for the *Apocalypse of Adam* was assembled by James.[3]

2. *Penitence of Adam*: This is proscribed by the Gelasian Decree, mentioned in the Armenian list of Samuel of Ani according to one text,[4] and possibly implied by the words of George Cedrenus, "Adam, in the 600th year, having repented,"[5] though significance of this latter reference is frequently denied.

3. *Testament of Adam*: A writing under this name occurs in a number of languages. Most important is the Syriac text, but versions also exist in Arabic, Ethiopic and Georgian. These are dealt with below in the relevant sections. The evidence for its Greek transmission is complicated.[6]

---

both in the exegetical and the iconographic spheres, but is little developed in the Adam literature. See, for example, Maguire, 1987, 363-373.

[3]   See above, Chapter 3, section 1.11; James, 1920, 1. See further discussion in Stone, 1982, 45-46 and Robinson, 1982, 8. A summary of this material may also be found in Morard, 1985, 7-10.

[4]   See above, Chapter 3, section 1.12. There are, of course, two surviving Armenian works bearing this or a similar title: see below section 6.

[5]   James, 1920, 2. See text in Stone, 1981a, *Translation*, ix. Denis, 1970, 9 notes that this is not the same as the work by that title in cod. Athos Batop. 84 which is actually part of a pseudo-Chrysostomian homily on Gen. 3. Although the material quoted by Cedrenus is attributed to Adam, it is by no means certain that his phrasing μετανοήσας actually implies that he is quoting a work called "Repentance of Adam." Moreover, the continuation of the passage reads δι' ἀποκαλύψεως which Renan equally saw as a possible hint at an "Apocalypse of Adam": see Renan, 1853, 431-32. In fact this argument is not convincing, although it seems to have been accepted recently by von Nordheim, 1980, 182-83.

[6]   We do not regard the *Transitus Mariae* as containing evidence for this work, see above Chapter 3, section 1.11: *pace* Robinson, 1982, 12. A his-

One part of this *Testament of Adam* is entitled "The Hours of Day and Night." In addition to the Syriac version, this part of *Testament of Adam* also exists in two forms in Greek. One form is attributed to Adam and the other to the noted first-century neo-Pythagorean philosopher, Apollonius of Tyana (or Tyanensis).[7] The form attributed to Apollonius was first published by M.R. James, the standard edition is by F. Nau, while yet a further text was published by F. Boll.[8] A recent diplomatic edition based on all known Greek manuscripts of this form of the text was published by Robinson who took BN grec 2419 as his base text.

In the Byzantine *Chronicle* of George Cedrenus, "The Hours of the Day" is included, and is related to Adam. The context in which it occurs in Cedrenus' *Chronicle* implies that in addition to "The Hours of the Day," which is quoted verbatim, a revelation to Adam took place which included information about the Watchers and the Flood, Adam's repentance, and the Incarnation, although the text of *Testament of Adam* dealing with these latter subjects is not cited word for word. This range of interests distinctly resembles what we find in the parts of the Syriac *Testament of Adam* additional to the "Hours of the Day and Night." Denis is of the view that this Greek fragment was drawn from an originally Jewish *Testament of Adam*, but reworked in a profoundly

---

tory of the identification of this work may be found in Levison, 1988, 22-28.

7   On the attribution of "The Hours of the Day and Night" see Stone, 1982, 44.

8   James first published the text of "The Hours of the Day and Night" from a Paris magical codex: James, 1893. A fuller edition is Nau, 1907, 2.1363-85 and see also Boll, 1908, 174-181. In his edition of George the Syncellus, Mosshammer, 1984, 10-11 gives the Greek text of the hours of the day and night. The material was already mentioned by G. Gaulmyn in his notes on Michael Psellus, *De Daemonum Operatione* (1615) which we have seen in *PG* 122.853-854. He cites extracts from the *Apotelesmata* for the hours of the night.

Christian fashion.[9] Robinson regards all the Greek evidence for *The Hours of the Day and Night* as deriving from Syriac.[10]

There may have been other writings by this title. A *Testament of the Protoplasts* is mentioned by Anastasius Sinaïta (*On the Hexaemeron* 7. 895 [PG 89.976]); see above, Chapter 3, section 1. M.R. James is of the opinion that *Testament of Adam* may also be referred to by Nicetas of Remesiana who mentions an *Inquisitio Abræ* which in his view is probably corrupt for *Dispositio Adæ*. i.e. *Testament of Adam*.[11]

4. *Life of Adam*: This is quoted by George the Syncellus in his *Chrono-graphy*, p. 5, and is chronological in character.[12] It is quite like *Testament of the Protoplasts* to which it is probably related.[13]

5. *Palaea Historica*: In addition to the works mentioned above, a chapter of the *Palaea Historica*, a retelling of sacred history, relates the story of the temptation, fall and expulsion of Adam, as well as the story

---

9   Denis, 1970, 11. Denis, *ibid* 12 discusses further testimonia to a *Testament* and a *Penitence of Adam*. It had partly been known, but not identified, since 1615, as is reported by Frey, 1928, 117: and see preceding note.

10   Robinson, 1982, 135-144.

11   So James, 1920, 3. Fabricius, 1713, 1.35-36 gives a number of medieval traditions describing Adam giving a testament. Frey, 1928, 123-124 cites a range of traditions relating to the use of Adamic testamentary materials in early Christianity. A *Testament of Adam* might also be referred to by the list of apocryphal books quoted by Samuel of Ani, see Chapter 3, section 1 above.

12   Text and Latin translation in Fabricius, 1713, 1.12-15.

13   In a private communication William Adler has commented: "Your argument that the *Life of Adam* and *Testament of the Protoplasts* are related is strengthened by the fact that Syncellus and Anastasius assert that the Christian chroniclers used them for the same reason (namely to account for the length of time spent by the protoplasts in Paradise). I would also add here that the citations which the chroniclers give from both sources appear to be expansions of *Jubilees* 3:1-9."

of Cain and Abel. This section of the *Palaea* is entitled Περὶ τοῦ Ἀδάμ.[14]

6. *Georgios Chumnos*: The Greek poem on Genesis and Exodus by the Cretan poet Georgios Chumnos (dated ca. 1500) contains extensive traditions about Adam and Eve and the antediluvian generations. He knows, for example, the tale of the second temptation, the second fall and the contract (χειρόγραφον) with Satan which does not occur in the primary Adam books. His sources for some of this material remain unclear, but it seems to have been known among the Greeks.[15] Thus, the same story is also reflected in various Greek liturgical compositions,[16] while a modern Greek retelling of this story of the χειρόγραφον of Adam was recorded early in the present century in Didimoteichon in Thrace and translated and discussed by Megas.[17] This indicates the continued life of this tradition among the Greeks: see further section 6, text 15 below. In an article, Saul Lieberman deals with the story of Satan's second deception of Adam and the contract between Adam and Satan as it is found in the poem of Georgios Chumnos and in the Slavonic *Vita Adam et Evae*. He claims to show that the form of the story known to Chumnos (whose poem is close to the Greek *Palaea* in other respects) is based on a misunderstanding of that found in Slavonic *Vita Adam et Evae*.[18]

2. In Latin

1. Tertullian in *On Penitence* has a passage that seems to imply that he knew (in the early third century) a book that contained hymns uttered

---

[14]   Vassiliev, 1893, 189-191; this has been discussed briefly by Flusser, 1971, 50. The *Palaea Historica* as a source of biblical legends was also discussed by Lieberman, 1972, 42-54.

[15]   Marshall, 1925. Megas, 1928, 311-312 discusses this text and points out the existence of two further manuscripts of it. It may be observed that there exists yet another, unpublished manuscript of this poem in St. Catherine's Monastery at Mt. Sinai. This is manuscript no. 1187: see Clark, 1952, 28-31.

[16]   Megas, 1928, 314-315.

[17]   Megas, 1928, 305-320.

[18]   Lieberman, 1972, 46-48: see also p. 72 above.

by Adam after his fall and repentance.[19] If Tertullian is indeed referring to an Adam book, it is hard to identify it with any of the above.

2. There is much additional Adam literature in Latin, and there are many references to the Adam story, much of it dependent on the Latin *Vita Adam et Evae*.[20] Murdoch draws a distinction between medieval Adam works of a "biblical" and of an "apocryphal" type. The former contain the biblical story treated as in the Latin *Vita Adam et Evae*, preceded by the fall of Lucifer, and followed by the story of Cain and Abel and of Cain's death at Lamech's hands, to which some other traditions are sometimes attached. Murdoch enumerates a number of Latin and vernacular treatments, including dramas, in this style. We forbear rehearsing them here, and refer the reader to Murdoch's instructive remarks.[21] This "biblical" tradition he traces back to the sixth century at least, while the "apocryphal" Adam tradition is chronologically later. The apocryphal works came into being subsequent to the establishment of the "biblical" epic and are prose or poetic expansions and embellishments of the Latin *Vita Adam et Evae*, both in Latin and in vernacular languages. Such versions occur in a variety of genres, rarely including drama, but many or most of them go back ultimately to rhymed form. These versions, after the penitence, include the Quest of Seth and the Holy Rood material, and often add the Lamech incident too. They are almost always related to a version of *Vita Adam et Evae*.[22]

---

[19]   James, 1920, 4.

[20]   Some indicative references to these may be found in the works cited above in Introduction 1, footnote 1 and in section 12 below.

[21]   Murdoch, 1976, 25-27.

[22]   Murdoch, 1976, 26-30. The Irish form of the material, in the *Saltair na Rann* is older than most other forms of it (*ibid*, 29-30). On pages 30-31 Murdoch notes some further sources, particularly in Celtic languages. Another Latin prose Holy Rood text was published by Mozley, 1930, 113-127. On Holy Rood material, see also section 12 below. Evans, 1966, 38-42 also discusses Adam's composition from elements. Originating supposedly in *2 Enoch* (pp. 38-39) this material is also known, it is claimed, in prose in *Solomon and Saturn*. Evans compares these texts with a Latin Anglo-Saxon ritual and similar texts in *Cursor Mundi* and in Middle English Adam texts (see section 12, below on these).

3. *Adam Octipartite:* This text also occurs in Old Irish and in Old Church Slavonic. See below, sections 9 and 10. The Latin text was published from a tenth century manuscript, and the tradition studied by M. Förster.[23] According to Förster, the Irish is translated from the Latin. Vernacular versions of this text occur in Old French, Middle Dutch,[24] Old Frisian,[25] and other languages. Versions of the text in Anglo-Saxon are related to the oldest Latin manuscript which goes back to the seventh century.[26] The origin of this document is to be sought in the Byzantine realm and Turdeanu, like Förster, is of the view that the Slavonic and the Latin versions go back to a Greek original.[27] In Latin, another tradition about the composition of Adam's name is associated with this text. This has wide ramifications and also occurs in some forms of the Latin *Vita Adam et Evae.*[28]

3. In Syriac

1. *The Cave of Treasures* is a history of biblical events down to the birth of Christ and Brock characterizes the work as "a christianized re-telling of the biblical narrative."[29] It commences from the creation and expul-

---

[23] Förster, 1907-08, 477-529. See also the discussion of this material by Turdeanu, 1981, 412-418.

[24] Förster, 1907-08, 483-486. Secondary forms occur in still further European vernaculars, see Förster, *ibid;* Turdeanu, 1981, 413.

[25] Förster, 1907-08, 491-492. He gives a number of texts in the Appendix to his article, pp. 522-529.

[26] See also discussion by Turdeanu, 1981, 416. A thorough recent study of the Old Irish and Old English texts is Tristram, 1975, 119-153.

[27] Turdeanu, 1981, 421.

[28] Förster, 1907-08, 514-520 investigates some parts of this theme. See also Tristram, 1975, 145-149. Further Latin Adam materials, connected with the above, including the "Octipartite Adam" traditions, the naming, and other features, are incorporated in a Latin dialogue book published by Förster, 1910, 342-348. The tradition of Adam's name is also discussed by Seymour, 1922, 126-127 and its occurrence in the *Hexaemeron* of Bede is noted by McNally, 1959, 26.

[29] See Brock, 1979, 227. Some general remarks on *Cave of Treasures* may be found in Baumstark, 1922, 95-96.

sion, follows biblical history in some detail to the time of Melchizedek,[30] and then provides an epitome of events down to the birth of Christ. It was originally composed in Syriac, and seems to have utilized extensive, and sometimes otherwise unknown Jewish sources. For instance, Brock discussed the tradition of the twin sisters of Cain and Abel as a good example of a Jewish tradition taken over by *Cave of Treasures*.[31] *Cave of Treasures* is one of the most significant of the secondary Adam books.

Cave of Treasures has been divided into the following parts:

1. Chapters 1-4: Hexaemeron, formation of Adam, Adam and Eve in the Garden; the expulsion.
2. Chapters 6-23: History of the forefathers down to the burial of Adam on Golgotha.
3. Chapters 24-27: Insertion of biblical history.
4. Chapters 28-34:10: From Abraham and Melchizedek to Moses.
5. Chapters 34:11-41: Later insertion.

---

[30] On attitudes to Melchizedek in *Cave of Treasures* and in other cognate sources, see Frey, 1928, 116-117.

[31] Brock, 1979, 228. A conspectus of the use of Jewish materials in Syriac literature is given by Brock, 1979, 212-232. Compare also the comments on the garments of Adam and Eve in Brock, 1982, 11-39, especially on pp. 14-15. This issue is discussed in connection with the Ethiopian exegetical tradition by Cowley, 1988, 65-70. An older study, adducing many parallels from Rabbinic literature is Bamberger, 1901, 29-54. He discusses traditions not only relating to the protoplasts, but to other parts of biblical history recounted by *Cave of Treasures*. Frey, 1928, 112-117 gives an extensive introduction to *Cave of Treasures*. He also discusses the burial traditions and other elements that are drawn from Jewish sources. He concludes from the Jewish material in *Cave of Treasures* and in *Conflict of Adam and Eve with Satan* that "il devait exister chez les Juifs, déjà antérieurement à Notre-Seigneur, un livre, rédigé en hébreu ou en araméen, qui complétait le récit biblique sur les premiers parents et les patriarches" (p. 114). His argument is that the two works, i.e. *Cave of Treasures* and *Conflict of Adam and Eve with Satan*, are interrelated, but that their relationship is not one of dependence in either direction, but of utilization of a common source document. *Non liquet* must be our present judgment on this matter until more extensive studies have been made of the apocryphal Adam traditions. Guerin, 1968, 13-14 also discusses traditions of Adam's burial according to Christian sources.

6. Chapters 42-43: Legends relevant to Sacred Scripture, Zerubbabel, Ezra, etc and the genealogy of the Virgin Mary.

7. Chapters 44-54: Apologetic, including generations from Adam to Christ with the names of wives.[32]

Cave of Treasures had an extensive influence on Oriental Christian literature. We cannot explore all of its ramifications here, but can only provide a few indications. In an article published in 1923-24, A. Götze studied the literary history of *Cave of Treasures* in Syriac, Arabic, and Ethiopic literature. He traces it from the Syriac *Pseudo-Dionysius the Areopagite* (first half of the sixth century), through the influential *Apocalypse of Pseudo-Methodius*, particularly in its presentation of the primordial history,[33] to the *Hexaemeron* of Pseudo-Epiphanius. It is subsequently utilized by the work entitled *Conflict of Adam and Eve with Satan* (discussed below, section 4), by Pseudo-Dionysius of Telmaḥrē (compiled ca. 775) and by 'al-Ya'qubi (ca. 889).[34] *The Book of the Bee* by Solomon of Bassorah (13th century) is dependent on *Cave of Treasures*.[35] The *Cave of Treasures* is introduced into the pseudo-Clementine literature, either as a narrative by Peter to Clement on the history of the world, or as a *Book of Mysteries*.[36]

---

[32]   Su-Min Ri,1987. In vol. 487, xix-xxiv he provides the analysis of the book which we have followed here.

[33]   See also Reinink, 1983, 46-64. He cites much further literature.

[34]   Götze, 1923, 51-94; idem, 1924, 53-71. In this extended study he also collates the various texts which he finds to be dependent on *Cave of Treasures* against the *Cave of Treasures* itself and presents extensive parallel texts. Denis, *Introduction (2ed; manuscript)* also deals in considerable detail with these later texts which draw upon *Cave of Treasures*.

[35]   Budge, 1886. A German translation is Schönfelder, 1866, (*non vidi*), but Budge comments that this translation "is based on the Munich MS. only, and is faulty in many places" (p. iii). See the discussion of this work in Brock, 1979, 229. Charlesworth, 1981, 91 notes that copies of Vatican Arabic MS 165 and BM Syr Ms. O.M.P. 5394, Add 25875 are preserved in the Pseudepigrapha Library at Duke University.

[36]   See Denis, 1970, 8. *The Book of Mysteries* is a compilation of the pseudo-Clementine *Recognitiones*, the *Cave of Treasures*, the *Testament of Adam*, and perhaps the *Apocalypse of Peter* (ibid). The relationship of *Kitāb al Magall* to the Arabic *Apocalypse of Peter* is also discussed by Gibson, 1901, vii. The book was first signalled by Assemanus, *Bibliotheca*

Date

Brock basically accepts the dates proposed by Götze, i.e. that the present form of the work is of the sixth century, but that it uses a prior document, dubbed "Urschatzhöhle," which existed by the fourth century (see above Chapter 2, section 2, where the date of *Cave of Treasures* is discussed).[37] In most Syriac sources, *Cave of Treasures* is attributed to "Saint Mar Ephraem"[38] and indeed, according to Bezold and Budge, it comes from the Ephraemite school. Other sources call its author "Modios," a corruption of "Methodius," reflecting the relationship of the work to the *Apocalypse of Pseudo-Methodius*.[39] There have been various speculations as to the place of composition, Edessa, the Syriac part of Mesopotamia, or an Egyptian monastic milieu have been suggested. Su-Min Ri prefers to leave the question open.[40]

Manuscripts and Editions

An edition of the Syriac with the Arabic version en face was prepared by Bezold based on four manuscripts (BM Add 25875; BM

Orientalis. He describes the work as "*Spelunca Thesaurorum,* hoc est, Chronicon e Scriptura desumptum ab Adam et Christum, et in partes VI. divisum, quarum unaquæque res gestas per mille annos complecitur" (1719-1728, 2.498).

[37] Brock, 1979, 227. Simon, 1970, 67-70 makes much of typological exegesis in the *Cave of Treasures.* He observes that these speculations tend "à démontrer que le christianisme est la religion originelle de l'humanité et, comme telle, beaucoup plus ancienne de le judaïsme" (p. 70). See also the article of Vogl, 1979, and see our observations in Introductory Remarks, note 3 above.

[38] Su-Min Ri, 1987. In vol. 487, xiii-xiv Su-Min Ri discusses the title, while on pp. xiv-xvi. he discusses the authorship.

[39] Bezold, 1888, ii, x. On "Modios," see note 32 above. On the importance of the incorporation of material from *Cave of Treasures* into the *Apocalypse of Pseudo-Methodius,* and its subsequent penetration into Latin Christendom, see Frey, 1928, 115-116 with a rich list of sources. It may be remarked that in an unpublished Armenian Adam work preserved in Erevan, Matenadaran Ms 10200 we have identified substantial extracts from pseudo-Methodius.

[40] Su-Min Ri, 1987, 487.xvi-xvii.

Add 7199, Sachau 131, Vat. Syr. 164).[41] Recently Su-Min Ri prepared a new edition based upon a collation of 19 manuscripts of the Syriac text.[42] These fell into two families, characterized as eastern and western. Bezold prepared an eclectic translation into German,[43] and another German translation was published by Riessler.[44] An English translation based on a Nestorian manuscript, BM Add 25875, was made by Budge.[45] *Cave of Treasures* is also extant in an Arabic translation from Syriac,[46] in an Ethiopic version which was translated from the Arabic[47]

---

[41] It has been pointed out that the Arabic text published by Bezold was in fact an extract from a larger work called *Apocalypse of Peter:* Cowley, 1988, 138 quoting de Lagarde. This Arabic *Apocalypse of Peter* has some relationship with Ethiopic *Qalementos*, see below.

[42] Su-Min Ri, 1987. In vol. 486, vi-xx the manuscripts used are set forth. In addition, the author refers to a total of 36 copies listed in the catalogues (p. vi), and himself provides a list of another seven manuscripts which were inaccessible or lost (p. xx). The author concludes that all the manuscripts derive from a single archetype and structures a stemma accordingly (486.xxiii-xxv). Some information on manuscripts and editions is also provided by Stegmüller, 1950, vol. 1, sections 76-76.8.

[43] Bezold, 1888.

[44] Riessler, 1928, 942-1013 with comments on pp. 1325-1326.

[45] Budge, 1927.

[46] Gibson, 1901, i-xxxi, 1-58 and Arabic text, pp. [1]-[56]. She observes that the Arabic text she publishes, from St. Catherine's Monastery, Arab. 508, fols. 89-141, is different in many details and often better than the Arabic text utilized by Bezold. For further Arabic bibliography of the *Cave of Treasures*, see Graf, 1944, 1.198-203. He distinguishes two different Arabic translations, an older one from a Monophysite perspective and a younger one included in the *Book of the Rolls* (p. 198-199). The text of Gibson is reproduced, accompanied by an Italian translation and commentary by Battista and Bagatti, 1980. This Arabic text is connected in some manuscripts with the so-called *Hexaemeron* of Pseudo-Epiphanius.

[47] Grébaut, 1911, 73; Nau, 1908, 3.216-219. See some further details in Denis, 1970, 8 n26. The translation was published by Grébaut in *ROC* under the title *Traduction de Qalémentos* (i.e. Clement) between 1911 and 1928. He observes that the work was already referred to by Dillmann, 1858, 185-226 (*non vidi*). The work, Grébaut reports, is made up of seven books, divided into two parts. The first relates the history of the world and the birth of the Virgin, as well as the revelation of heavenly secrets; the

(apparently produced between 750 and 760),[48] in Coptic (see below, section 5), and in Georgian (see below, section 7).

2. *Testament of Adam*: This work is composed of three fragments, *Hours of the Day and Night*, *Adam's Prophecy to Seth* and *Angelology*. *Hours of the Day and Night* lists the various elements of creation and the hour on which they praise God. *Angelology* mentions the heavenly hosts and the names of the various classes of the angels, while *Adam's Prophecy to Seth* foretells events down to the flood, including the corruption of the earth and the fate of Adam's remains. The literary history and structure of this work have been debated for a century and a half.

The relationship of the first fragment, *Hours of the Day and Night*, to *Testament of Adam* has been under discussion since the time of Renan.[49] Denis opines that it was drawn from the original *Testament of Adam* (which he apparently considers a Greek work), while *Adam's Prophecy to Seth* was taken from *Cave of Treasures* or from a "livre d'Adam primitif" (whatever that might have been).[50] E. von Nordheim pays especial attention to testamentary elements in *Adam's Prophecy to Seth*. He notes its relationship to Adam traditions in the *Chronicle* of Eutychius of Alexandria.[51] In his study, Robinson insists that the first and second parts were written in Syriac in the second or, more probably the third century,[52] perhaps drawing on older sources.[53] He main-

---

second treats the laws and orders of the church (Grébaut, 1911, 72-73). This document is discussed by Cowley, 1988, 136-140.

[48]   Su-Min Ri, 1987, 487.16.

[49]   Renan, 1853. See also Reinink, 1972, 387-388. This fragment was also discussed above in connection with the secondary Adam writings in Greek.

[50]   See Denis, 1970, 28.

[51]   Von Nordheim, 1980, 171-184. He deals with the testamentary material on pp. 172-176 and quotes the text of Eutychius on p. 176. He finds the typological importance of the time of Adam's death or expulsion, found in both Eutychius and in *Cave of Treasures*, to be an indication of an early Jewish element, turned to anti-Jewish polemic by *Cave of Treasures* (p. 176). On pp. 178-179 he attempts to reconstruct the structure of his hypothetical Jewish *Testament of Adam*.

[52]   Robinson, 1982, 148-153.

tains that *Hours of the Day and Night* and *Adam's Prophecy to Seth*, although perhaps originating in different sources, were "compatible enough to have been drawn together into a single document." Moreover, he argues that *Hours of the Day and Night* is a Jewish composition.[54] The place of *Angelology* in *Testament of Adam* was called into doubt by Migne and by Frey[55] and Robinson, too, regards *Angelology* as a later composition which knew *Hours of the Day and Night*.[56]

Testament of Adam is clearly related in content to *Cave of Treasures*, and occurs together with it in certain language traditions, such as Arabic and Georgian, but not in Syriac. It has been questioned whether *Testament of Adam* was originally part of *Cave of Treasures* or even of the *Urschatzhöhle*. Reinink observes that *Testament of Adam* is analogous to *Cave of Treasures* in some ways and in others differs from it. Moreover, although it is transmitted in the Arabic forms of *Cave of Treasures*, in Syriac it is independent of that work.[57] He concludes, therefore, that it was an originally independent work, which was fragmentary in character and was included secondarily into the Arabic *Cave of Treasures* tradition.

The question of date has scarcely been broached. As noted above, Robinson would date *Testament of Adam* to the second or third century, while Charlesworth suggests late second century C.E. with tradition of conflict over the sister reflecting early Syriac asceticism.[58]

---

[53]   Robinson, 1982, 135-144. This argument, based on the supposed parallel in *Apocalypse of Elijah*, does not seem convincing (150-151).

[54]   Robinson, 1982,159-160: see particularly p. 145. In a separate article he seeks for affinities between the *Hours of the Day and Night* and the Angelic Liturgy from Qumran: Robinson, 1985, 105-110. One of his points of similarity, the noise of the wings of the angels, surely goes back to Ezek 1:24.

[55]   Migne, 1856-58, 1.293, note 174; Frey, 1928, 120-121.

[56]   Robinson, 1982, 146-148.

[57]   Reinink, 1972, 390-91. This point was made already in large part by Götze, 1923, 92-94.

[58]   Charlesworth, 1981, 91.

Testament of Adam is found in Syriac, but it also survives in Greek (see above, section 1), Arabic,[59] Ethiopic[60] and Georgian.[61] It was first published in Syriac by Renan, subsequently by Bezold, and then re-edited on a broader manuscript basis by Kmosko who distinguished three recensions of the Syriac text, each preserved in two manuscripts.[62] Most recently S.E. Robinson published a Syriac text based on eight manuscripts with an English translation, introduction and commentary. He regards Recension 1 (Ms BL add. 14,624 and Vatican syr. 58) as being the best surviving form of the text. He also gives an insightful history of research into this work.[63] A French translation was published by Migne and a German one by Riessler.[64]

3. *Other Jewish Traditions in Syriac Sources:* Many other traditions of Jewish origin which relate to the protoplasts are embedded in the Syriac tradition. Only a few examples can be offered here. Brock observes that

---

[59] Important information had already been published in Renan, 1853, 427-71 and he presented an Arabic text of *The Testament of Adam*. A further Arabic text was published by Bezold, 1906, 893-912 and another by Gibson, 1901, 13-17. Bezold discusses the textual affinities of the Arabic version: Bezold, 1906, 910. One Armenian translation of *Hours of the Day and Night* (see below, section 6, no. 22) depends on an Arabic text of a different type to that published in the works just cited: see Stone, 1982, 41. Another previously unknown Armenian version of the *Hours of the Day and Night* has recently been identified. This second Armenian version is related to the form of the text found in *The Testament of Adam*.

[60] Published by Bezold, 1906. He is of the view that the Ethiopic text derives from the Arabic, with no independent connection either with Syriac or with Greek (p. 910). See already the comments on this by Migne, 1856-58, 1.390 quoting a communication of Dillmann.

[61] See below in section 7 concerning the Georgian version.

[62] Renan, 1853. Kmosko, 1907, 2. 1309-60, 1393-1410. On these manuscripts, see also Stone, 1982, 39-40. English translations in Budge, 1907, 242-248 and in Gibson, 1901, 13-17. The contents of the text are discussed in some detail by Frey, 1928, 118-120. A French translation was included by Migne, 1856-58, 1.289-98.

[63] Robinson, 1982. See also Charlesworth, 1981, 272-273. Robinson also translated the work in Charlesworth, 1983, 1.989-995.

[64] Migne, 1856-58, 1.289-298; Riessler, 1928, 1084-1090 and comments on p. 1332.

the Pešiṭṭa to Gen 4:8a has Abel killed in a valley, which is apparently related to the traditions of the Sethites and Cainites.[65] He also finds a development of the Sethite tradition in the Syriac (and Greek) chronicles
tradition, which connects the *benê 'Elohîm* "the sons of God" of Genesis 6 with the Sethites.[66] Likewise, the tradition of the robe of light which
Adam and Eve lost with the fall, which is widespread in Syriac sources, is
drawn from Jewish origins,[67] while a notion of Abel's ascent to heaven
which also probably came from Jewish sources, is apparently the object
of Ephraem's polemic in his *Commentary on Genesis* 3.5.[68] V. Aptowitzer argues that the legend of Adam's remains and their fate after his
death until their eventual interment at Golgotha is of Jewish origin. His
chief source for this material is *Cave of Treasures* and he also uses
some data from *Conflict of Adam and Eve.*[69]

4. In Ethiopic

1. *Conflict of Adam and Eve with Satan*: This writing deals with a series
of conflicts between the protoplasts and Satan, with the life of Adam
and Eve, and briefly with the history of Israel down to the birth of
Christ. The work shows a particular interest in Seth and Melchizedek. It is
is a Christian work translated from Arabic into Ethiopic later than the
seventh century.[70] The Ethiopic text has been published and translated

---

[65]   See Brock, 1979, 217.

[66]   Brock, 1979, 230-231. On this see further: Adler, 1989, 114-121,137-138.
       Compare also the observations of Migne, 1856-58, 2.42-43. The same idea
       is discussed as it occurs in the hymns of Ephraem Syrus by Kronholm,
       1978, 150 and 163-170.

[67]   Brock, 1979, 221-223.

[68]   Brock, 1979, 226-227. See also Kronholm, 1978, 215-224.

[69]   See Aptowitzer, 1924, 145-162. A *Life of Abel*, originally composed in
       Syriac and surviving in that language, has been published by Brock, 1974,
       467-492. He regards it as written in the fifth or sixth century C.E.

[70]   This date is proposed by Frey, 1928, 111. Others would set it as late as
       the eleventh century. An extensive survey of all the Ethiopian literature
       dealing with the creation material is to be found in Cowley, 1988, 113-142.
       In J. Simon, 1941, 290-291 there is a good deal of bibliographical and

into English, French and German, while the Arabic remained unedited until recently.[71] This work is clearly related to *Cave of Treasures* and contains the tradition about the cave. It is also connected with *Testament of Adam*.[72] Frey is of the opinion that while the first part of the work used Jewish traditions such as *Jubilees*, Latin *Vita Adam et Evae* and *Apocalypse of Moses*, the second part is definitely Christian in character.[73] Turdeanu argues that this work is, in terms of the themes discussed, closest of all the secondary Adam literature to the primary Adam writings. He notes the following points: (1) The wrath of the animals against Adam and Eve because of their sin; (2) the contract; (3) the spiritual purification in water;[74] (3) the forty days' of purification; (5) the second temptation of Eve; and (6) the angelic intercession on

---

other information about development of Adam materials in the Ethiopic tradition.

[71] Ethiopic: see Trumpp, 1881, 1-172; Dillmann, 1853, 1-144. An English translation and commentary may be found in Malan, 1882. A French translation also exists, in Migne, 1856-58, 1.290-388. In Ethiopic the work is associated with the pseudo-Epiphanian *Hexaemeron* which was published by Trumpp in the same Bavarian Academy series in 1882 (see Trumpp, 1882); see also on this Haffner, 1921-22, 91-145. The Hexaemeric literature in Ethiopic is discussed in considerable detail by Cowley, 1988, 122-128. He discusses the Pseudo-Epiphanian *Hexaemeron* on p. 124. These texts are also considered and their relationship to *Cave of Treasures* defined by Götze, 1923, 1924. We are dependent on Denis for the judgments as to date, etc. given above. Concerning the Arabic, see section 5, below.

[72] See, e.g., the comments of Budge, 1907, 12-14. He published an English translation of the Ethiopic version in *ibid*, 242-248. The text was published, of course, by Bezold, 1906 (see above). Substantial introductory comments on this work are to be found in Frey, 1928, 106-111: see also above, section 3, where the *Testament of Adam* and its versions are discussed.

[73] See Frey, 1928, 110. He discusses in particular the centrality for this part of the work of the tradition of the burial of Adam's skull at Golgotha. He enquires, however, whether there might have existed a Jewish tradition of Adam's burial in Jerusalem, on which see the discussion of Aptowitzer, 1924.

[74] Turdeanu, 1981, 78 deals with possible connections of this idea with Manichean praxis and concepts. The analysis of the two works covers pages 77-80 in his book.

Adam's behalf. He would explain this shared material by common dependence on Adamic legends and not by direct literary dependance.

2. *Testament of Adam* also exists in Ethiopic, and this version is discussed in the preceding section.

3. *Mäṣḥafä Adam* or "Book of Adam" referred to by Cowley and Teferu as existing in manuscripts might well be *Conflict of Adam and Eve*.[75]

5. In Arabic

1. The Arabic versions of *Cave of Treasures* and of *Testament of Adam* are dealt with in section 3 above.

2. An additional writing in Arabic with close connections with *Cave of Treasures* is the *Hexaemeron* of Pseudo-Epiphanius. After the description of the cosmogony, this work deals with the history of Adam and Eve and their expulsion from Paradise. This has been claimed to be the Arabic text of the work known in Ethiopic as *Conflict of Adam and Eve* or *Book of Adam and Eve* (see preceding section), but this point remains unclear, for the two works are not identical in Ethiopic. It remains to be determined whether this work was composed in Arabic or whether it was translated into Arabic from another language.[76] Denis is of the view that the Arabic was composed on the basis of, or translated from a Syriac text perhaps derived from *Cave of Treasures*.[77]

3. *Conflict of Adam and Eve with Satan*. The Arabic text has been edited by Battista and Bagatti, based upon nine manuscripts.[78] These

---

[75]   Cowley and Teferu, 1971, manuscript #18. Grébaut, 1914, 19 cites an Ethiopic story of Adam and Eve found in an *Introduction to the Four Gospels*.

[76]   See Graf, 1944, 201. For further bibliography and manuscripts, *ibid*, 202-203. The text is discussed in some detail by Haffner, 1921-22; compare also Götze, 1923, 1924. As observed, this Arabic text remains unpublished.

[77]   Denis, *Introduction (2nd ed. manuscript)*. He also deals with use of this work in antiquity.

[78]   Battista, and Bagatti, 1982. On the manuscripts, see pp. 14-16. An earlier report on this material was given by Bagatti, 1980. Grébaut, 1913, 432-441

scholars assume a common Jewish source (in Hebrew) for material shared by this work and the primary Adam books.[79]

6. In Armenian

There are very extensive Adam writings preserved in Armenian. The first modern publication of some of these writings was by S. Yovsēp'ianc' in his collection of Armenian apocryphal writings which appeared in Venice in 1898.[80] His collection was translated into English by J. Issaverdens[81] and into German by E. Preuschen.[82] A new edition of this corpus of material was prepared recently by L. Lipscomb in which he includes further recensions of certain of the writings and, after recollating the manuscripts, is able to fill in some major lacunae.[83] In addition there exist rather a lot of further works, some of which have been edited and others of which are currently under study.[84] The following compositions have been noted so far in the published literature or have been edited for publication by the writer from manuscripts.[85]

---

also published a partial edition of this text. The Arabic text was also discussed by Haffner, 1921-22, 93-94. For further details, see Denis, 1970, 9. The whole matter of texts and affinities of these works in Syriac, Arabic and Ethiopic is complicated, and a most helpful chart has been prepared by Cowley, 1988, 140.

[79]   Battista and Bagatti, 1982, 27.

[80]   Yovsēp'ianc', 1898.

[81]   Issaverdens, 1901.

[82]   Preuschen, 1900, 163-252 and *separatim.*

[83]   Lipscomb, 1990.

[84]   Lists of the Armenian Adam literature may be found in the following sources: Anasyan, 1959, 1.s.v.; Stone, 1981b, 2.460-464. There is an update of the list given in that article in Stone, 1984, 79-91. For the sake of consistency the numbers of those lists are preserved in the following which explains the inclusion in it of the primary Adam work, *Penitence of Adam* and the Armenian translation of *Apocalypse of Moses,* which is called *Book of Adam* in Armenian.

[85]   There are a number of further Armenian works dealing with Adam and Eve, but they are known to us at present only in manuscript. A number of them will be included in our forthcoming work, *Armenian Apocrypha: Relating to the Protoplasts* (Jerusalem: Israel Academy of Sciences and

1-4. *The Cycle of Four Works:* This composition is made up of four parts, which are enumerated here and which are usually listed with separate titles. Together they provide a conspectus of antediluvian history from creation down to the death of Adam. The best edition is now that of Lipscomb.[86] Two recensions of this work exist, the second of which was made known to western scholarship for the first time by Lipscomb.[87] The constituent parts of *Cycle of Four Works* are the following:

1. *History of the Creation and Transgression of Adam:* Yovsēp'ianc', 307-311; Issaverdens, 39-45; Preuschen, 29-30. Lipscomb, Recension 1, 108-127; Recension 2, text 241-245, translation 261-266.

2. *History of the Expulsion of Adam from the Garden:* Yovsēp'ianc', 312-314; Issaverdens, 47-51; Preuschen, 31-33; Lipscomb, Recension 1, 128-141; Recension 2, text 246-248, translation 267-269.

3. *History of Abel and Cain, Sons of Adam:* Yovsēp'ianc', 314-319; Issaverdens, 53-61; Preuschen, 33-36; Lipscomb, Recension 1, 142-171; Recension 2, text 249-254, translation 270-275; further collations, Stone, *Patriarchs and Prophets,* 33-38.

4. *Concerning the Good Tidings of Seth:* Yovsēp'ianc', 319-324; Issaverdens, 63-70; Preuschen, 36-40; Lipscomb, Recension 1, 172-205; Recension 2, text 255-260, translation 276-282.

Manuscripts and Recensions of the Cycle of Four Works

Lipscomb uses the following witnesses to Recension 1:

Y   Venice, Mechitarist, Old no. 729, undated. This manuscript was also the basis of Yovsēp'ianc''s text. Lipscomb did not have a photographic copy of the manuscript and he used the printed text. The manuscript has a complete text of *Cycle of Four*

Humanities). Robinson, 1982, 17 refers to an Armenian version of *Cave of Treasures.* No evidence for the existence of this is known to us.

[86]   Lipscomb, 1990, 16-20. He drew information on unavailable manuscripts chiefly from Anasyan, 1959, 1.240-241.

[87]   For bibliographical details of these editions and translations, see below in the discussion of the manuscripts and editions of the work.

Works, including homilies following each of its parts. The homilies were not published by Yovsēp'ianc'.

A   Erevan, Matenadaran, No. 682, fols. 96v-101r, undated. The manuscript contains three of the four parts of *Cycle of Four Works*, omitting only the first of them. It also contains homilies between the works.

B   New York, H.P. Kraus Rare Books and Manuscripts, MS VT915, fols. 4v-23v, dated 1662. This copy lacks the first third of the first part and the title of *History of Abel and Cain*. In *Concerning the Good Tidings of Seth* it has a long addition. It contains homilies.

C   Erevan, Matenadaran, No. 2126, fols. 81r-83r. This manuscript contains the final four fifths of *History of Abel and Cain*. Collations of this manuscript were also published separately by Stone.[88]

D   London, British Library, Ms Harl. Or. 5459, fols. 2v-12v, dated 1698. Full text of *Cycle of Four Works* with no homilies.

Lipscomb also knew of two further witnesses to Recension 1, which were not available to him, viz.:

F   Venice, Mechitarist, No. 262, fols. 163v-167v. Contains only *History of Abel and Cain*.

G   Erevan, Matenadaran, No. 4618, fols 138r-141v, 16-18th century. This seems to contain only *History of Abel and Cain* and *Concerning the Good Tidings of Seth*.

Lipscomb also published an edition and a first translation of Recension 2 of *Cycle of Four Works*. The text he drew from the following old printed source:

---

[88]   Stone, 1982, 33-38.

Z   *Ակիզբն Գրոց որ կոչի ժողովածու* (Constantinople: 1717), fols. 1-
        42.[89]

He also knew of one manuscript of this recension, but did not have access to it, viz.:

T   Tiflis, Kekelidze Institute of Manuscripts, No. 47, fols. 7r ff.

To these known witnesses to the two recensions, we may now add the following information. Lipscomb's codex C, Erevan, Matenadaran, No.
2129 also contains *Concerning the Good Tidings of Seth*. Erevan, Matenadaran, No. 7231 and Erevan, Matenadaran, No. 6340 contain most or
all of the *Cycle of Four Works*.[90] The text of Matenadaran, No. 2129 resembles Recension 1, while the character of the other two manuscripts
has not yet been determined. It is most likely that a further search will
uncover yet more copies of this work.

5. *The History of the Repentance of Adam and Eve:* This survives in a
single, known manuscript, i.e. Erevan, Matenadaran, No. 1521, fols. 66r-
69r, dated 1404. A manual copy of it was made by F.C. Conybeare and
presented to the Venice Mechitarists, so it was included in
Yovsēp'ianc''s book. Its sources included the Armenian *Book of Adam*,
an alternative or earlier form of *Cycle of Four Works*, and the
Armenian text of Genesis.[91] This work may be found in Yovsēp'ianc',
325-330; Issaverdens, 71-80; Preuschen, 41-46; Lipscomb, 210-233.

6. *Adam's Words to Seth:* This document deals with the quest of Seth,
but is different from the *Adam Fragments* which also deal with the same
topic (see below, nos. 9-11). It may be found in Yovsēp'ianc', 331-332;
Issaverdens, 81-83; Preuschen, 46-47; Lipscomb, 206-209. A second English translation is given in Stone, 1982, 12-13.

7. *Death of Adam:* This may be an excerpt from a Greek "rewritten
Bible" other parts of which might also have survived in Armenian. In

---

[89]   This was subsequently reprinted thrice: Constantinople 1730 (fols. 1-39);
        Constantinople 1747 (fols. 1-36), and Constantinople 1793 (fols. 1-35).

[90]   Collations of all these texts will be included in the author's forthcoming
        volume *Armenian Apocrypha: Relating to the Protoplasts*.

[91]   Lipscomb, 1990, 36-38.

structure it is a very brief cycle of the expulsion, the birth of the children of Adam and Eve, and, in greater detail, the visions seen by Seth and Eve of Adam's death and burial. This work may be found in Yovsēp'ianc', 24-26; Issaverdens, 85-89; Preuschen, 24-26. Lipscomb did not publish an edition of this text, since it had recently been re-edited by Stone,[92] who also produced two studies on it.[93] Stone's edition was based on the following manuscripts:

A   Yovsēp'ianc''s text, drawn from Venice, Mechitarist, no. 729.
B   Jerusalem, Armenian Patriarchate, No. 372, pp. 312-5, dated 1347.
C   Jerusalem, Armenian Patriarchate, No. 642, pp. 185-7, dated 1623.
D   Jerusalem, Armenian Patriarchate, No. 1488, pp. 613-7, dated 1620.
E   Jerusalem, Armenian Patriarchate, No. 1529, pp. 275-80, dated 1648.

Two further copies are known to exist, Erevan, Matenadaran, No. 711, of 18th century and Matenadaran no. 10200.[94]

8. *The Book of Adam:* This has been discussed above, Chapter 1, section 1. It is the Armenian version of the *Apocalypse of Moses* and is included in the present list for technical reasons as noted above.

9. *Adam Fragment 1:* This and the next two texts deal with the quest of Seth for the branch of the tree of life. They are similar, but not identical. *Adam Fragment 1* has been edited by Stone from two manuscripts.[95]

C   Jerusalem, Armenian Patriarchate, No. 642, p. 188, dated 1623
E   Jerusalem, Armenian Patriarchate, No. 1529, pp. 280-1, dated 1648.

---

92   Stone, 1982, 15-21.

93   Stone, 1982, 15-21; Stone, 1966, 283-291. A commentary is also included there.

94   See Eganyan, Zeyt'unyan, and Ant'abyan, 1965, 1.389 for no. 711. The collations of Erevan, Matenadaran 10200 will be included in the forthcoming work by Stone, *Armenian Apocrypha: Relating to the Protoplasts.*

95   Stone, 1982, 2-11.

A new copy has recently been discovered in Erevan, Matenadaran, No. 10200, p. 405.[96]

10. *Adam Fragment 2:* The text has been edited by Stone from Erevan, Matenadaran, No. 2126, p. 234, dated 1660.[97]

11. *Adam Fragment 3:* This unpublished fragment is noted by H. Anasyan to exist in Erevan, Matenadaran, No. 3358, fol. 3v.[98] The manuscript is dated to 1687 and 1746.[99]

12. *The Penitence of Adam:* This is the primary Adam work discussed above in Chapter 1, section 4. It is included here for technical reasons.

13. *Concerning Adam, His Sons and Grandsons:* A synopsis and preliminary study of this work have been published, but a critical edition of the text is still awaited.[100] It contains a paraphrase of the biblical text in chapters 4 and 5 of Genesis, followed by parallel and expansionary traditions connected with it. It is particularly related to *Repentance of Adam and Eve* and less closely with *Cycle of Four Works.* It was studied on the basis of one manuscript, and a number of other copies have since come to light. In addition, the work was printed quite a long time ago in hagiographical collections, but those printings have had no impact on the scholarly world. The preparation of a new edition is currently underway.[101]

14. *Concerning the Contract between Adam and Satan:* This work, preserved in Jerusalem, Armenian Patriarchate, No. 840, is now known to be part of the document entitled *Questions* which will be mentioned below. It is no longer to be regarded as an independent writing, as was done

---

[96]   Collations of this will be published in Stone, *Armenian Apocrypha: Relating to the Protoplasts.*

[97]   Stone, 1982, 2-11.

[98]   Anasyan, 1959, 1.243.

[99]   See Eganyan, Zeyt'unyan, and Ant'abyan, 1965, 1.995-996.

[100]   Stone, 1984, 79-91.

[101]   To be published by Stone, *Armenian Apocrypha: Relating to the Protoplasts.*

previously.[102] The tradition referred to in this text is complex and of wide and significant spread. It is notable that, in addition to the rather extensive material in Armenian, in the Arabic and Ethiopic *Conflict of Adam and Eve with Satan* and in the Slavonic *Vita Adam et Evae*, it is also known in Greek. Thus it is to be found in the medieval Greek poem of Georgios Chumnos[103] and in the modern Greek tale recorded by Megas.[104] Marshall, in his translation of Chumnos, does not know of Greek sources for the tale, and refers instead to the Slavonic *Vita Adam et Evae* for it.[105] See further above, Chapter 1, section 3 for a discussion of the Slavonic evidence and development of this theme.

15. *The Letter Sent to Adam by God:* This short text exists in Erevan, Matenadaran, No. 2111, fol. 229v. It relates that God gave Adam a letter promising redemption in the sixth millennium which was transmitted to Cyrus and then to the Magi.[106] Another writing, apparently with the same tale, is to be found in Venice, Mechitarist, No. 240, 10v-11r, and the same tradition recurs in certain Armenian New Testament apocrypha.

16. *Poem on the Fall of Adam:* This short composition occurs in Erevan, Matenadaran, No. 711, fols. 3v-4r.[107]

17. *The Story of Adam and Eve and the Incarnation:* This work is known from three manuscripts, two in the Matenadaran in Erevan and one in the Bibliothèque Nationale in Paris, none of which is particularly old. It is centred around the theme of Adam and Eve's contract with Satan, and concludes with the story of the Incarnation in which that contract was annulled: see above, no. 14 in the present list on that subject.

---

102 Stone, 1982, 463, following Anasyan, 1959, 1.242.

103 Marshall, 1925, 1-7. See further, section 1 above. See also Chapter 1, section 3 above.

104 Megas, 1928, 305-320.

105 See below, section 10 where further complex traditions associated with this text are discussed.

106 Stone, 1982, 463-4 and Anasyan, 1959, 243.

107 Together with items 17-21 in this list, it is currently being readied for publication by the writer and will be included in his work *Armenian Apocrypha: Relating to the Protoplasts*.

Each manuscript contains a recension of the work so different from the two others that they have to be published in a synoptic edition. The chief sources of the document appear to be the Bible and *Cycle of Four Works*.

18. *Adam and His Grandsons:* This work occurs in Jerusalem, Armenian Patriarchate, No. 1529. The manuscript was copied in 1648. The work outlines the history of the antediluvian generations, the names of the wives of the patriarchs, and certain other chronological matters. This text is replete with chronological details, which are analogous to a number of other documents. Two such other lists of eras of the world may be mentioned, both in Erevan, Matenadaran, No. 9100: one we have entitled *Concerning the Six Millennia* and the other, *The Eleven Eras*.[108]

19. *Adam Story 1:* This brief text, like the two that ensue, is to be found in Erevan, Matenadaran, No. 9100. It tells the story of the second fall of Adam and the contract with Satan, as well as certain details concerning Enoch and other patriarchs.

20. *Adam Story 2:* This is a short text, from the same manuscript, which tells the story of the Fall, with special interest in chronological matters.

21. *Question:* The text with this strange title is a history from the time of the antediluvian fathers down to the eschaton. It is not very long, but contains a range of interesting traditions, including that to Nebrot' (Nimrod), that of Maniton who was Noah's fourth son, and others. It includes material from the *Apocalypse of Pseudo-Methodius* and is also to be found in Matenadaran no. 9100.

22. *Hours of the Day and Night:* This work, part of *Testament of Adam* occurs in one form in Armenian under the name of Apollonius of Tyana.[109] Another Armenian translation exists of the type of text to be

---

[108]   These texts will be published, together with other such material, in the forthcoming *Armenian Apocrypha: Relating to the Protoplasts.*

[109]   See Stone, 1982, 39-80.

found in the *Testament of Adam*.[110] It is discussed above in sections 1 and 3.

23. *The Descendants of Adam:* We have given this title to the fragmentary writing which forms the first part of *The Biblical Paraphrases*. The actual title has been lost from the manuscript, but the document clearly dealt with the antediluvian generations.[111]

There have been a few studies of the Armenian Adam books. They have usually entertained the possibility that this rich Armenian tradition contained ancient elements, many times claimed to be gnostic.[112] An assessment of the representation of Seth in the better known Armenian Adam books, however, concluded that, at most (and that not very probably) *Death of Adam* might be reusing some Sethian gnostic traditions. No other evidence appeared for gnostic features of the Armenian works.[113] Of greater significance is the history of the traditions embodied in these works: here the evidence that has emerged so far indicates that the Armenians had available some very ancient traditions, to which on occasion, these Armenian documents provide the sole later attestation. This matter will have to be assessed differently in the case of each work, since the different documents vary from one another greatly in both their character and their originality. A third observation is that the role of this literature and these traditions within Armenian literary and religious culture is very significant and must be the subject of a special study. The extensive Armenian medieval poetic accounts of creation and the primordial history are clearly indebted to

---

[110] This will be published in the forthcoming *Armenian Apocrypha: Relating to the Protoplasts*.

[111] Stone, 1982, 84-87.

[112] This was the position maintained, for example, by Preuschen, 1900. A similar stance was taken by Cardona, 1967, 645-648. Preuschen's position was challenged early on by Kabisch, 1905, 111-121. Kabisch's other arguments on provenance do not seem convincing. Liechtenhan, 1902, 222-223 also refutes Preuschen's position.

[113] Stone, 1982, 471.

this apocryphal literature, and the matter merits further, more detailed, investigation.[114]

7. In Georgian

1. *The Cycle of Four Works*: An interesting report on Georgian Adam books was published by W. Lüdtke in 1919-20.[115] He observes that the Adam books in Georgian mentioned in the older article by A. Chachanov[116] are related to the material published by Yovsēp'ianc' in Armenian and that these Georgian books constitute a Georgian version of *Cycle of Four Works*.

Tarchnishvili, in his work on the history of Georgian ecclesiastical literature, which in turn reflects the magistral study of K. Kekelidze, reports the existence of the following writings:

2. *Georgian Life of Adam and Eve*: This is presumably what Tarchnishvili means by the title "Georgian Adam Book." This is the primary Adam book discussed above in Chapter 1, section 5.

3. *The Cave of Treasures*: This book appears under the title "Report of our Holy Father Ephraem, Commentary on the Creation of the Heaven, the Earth and of Adam." This Georgian version of *Cave of Treasures* was made in the eleventh century.[117] It is identical with the "Book of Nebrot'" often mentioned in Georgian historical writings.[118]

---

[114]   See for example the poems translated by Russell, 1987, 165-187.

[115]   Lüdtke, 1919-20, 155-168.

[116]   Chachanov, 1894, 35-49; Chachanov, 1895, 165-170. He also points out that the *Primary History of Georgia* (*K'art'lis C'hoverba*) contains some Adamic material.

[117]   Su-Min Ri, 1987, 487.16, cf. Avalichvili, 1928, 392.

[118]   See Tarchnishvili, *Geschichte*, 335-336. See further Lüdtke, 1919-20, 161-162 on this work. The identification of the *Cave of Treasures* in Georgian was made by Džavachov, 1905, 26. A translation is given by Avalichvili, 1928, 381-405. His work was also published *separatim*. He regards the Georgian as a translation of an earlier stage of the text than has survived in Syriac. Some general comments on the Apocrypha in Georgian may be found in Blake, 1925, 61. An earlier publication relating to the Georgian Adam books was: Džanašvili, 1909, 19-44.

4. *Testament of Adam*: Tarchnishvili records that in Hobi Ms no. 6 of year 1813 are found "Concerning the Twelve Hours of the Day"and "Concerning the Twelve Hours of the Night" which are together surely the first part of *Testament of Adam*.[119] A French translation of the Georgian text was published by Avalichvili.[120] He observed that the text is introduced by a passage drawn from *Cave of Treasures* and is followed by an apocalyptic passage related to, but not identical with "The Christian Apocalypse" which is also part of the Syriac *Testament of Adam*.[121]

5. The same manuscript contains three further compositions, viz. "Expulsion of Adam and Eve from Paradise," "Creation of Heaven and Earth," and "Book Concerning the Creation."[122] The identification of the first two of these is not certain,[123] but perhaps the third work is the same as the Georgian version of the *Cave of Treasures*.

8. In Coptic

1. Poirier has published a fragmentary Coptic version of *Cave of Treasures*. He identified this on two papyrus leaves in the collection of the Pierpont Morgan Library in New York. They came from Fayoum and have been dated to the ninth century. Poirier concludes that these leaves derive from a full translation of *Cave of Treasures* into Coptic, to which no other witness is known. In general, the text resembles that of the Syriac, but it has been adapted, in proper names for example, to the norms of the Coptic Bible. The language from which the translation was made cannot be determined.[124]

---

[119]   Lüdtke, 1919-20, also translated some excerpts from this.

[120]   Avalichvili, 1927-1928, 402-405.

[121]   See also Stone, 1982, 42.

[122]   Tarchnishvili, 1955, pp. 335-336. He also refers to H. Ms. 1378 fols 1-24 which contains a number of "Schöpfungsapokryphen."

[123]   Perhaps they are parts of the Georgian version of the *Cycle of Four Works*.

[124]   Poirier, 1983, 415-423.

2. Above, in Chapter 1, section 6, reference was made to the apparent rewriting of part of the primary Adam books in the *Discourse on Abbatôn* by Timothy, Archbishop of Alexandria. This document relates, among other things, the story of creation, the fall, and the descent of Christ into Hades. It also contains some Adam traditions differing from those to be found in the primary Adam books.

3. The underwriting of a four-page Coptic palimpsest in Vatican, copt. 65 gives part of a story about the revolt of Satan against God and Michael's fight against him. Satan is also denoted as Mastema; he refuses to worship God, the Cross or to honor Adam. God sends Michael to fight him and invests Michael with wondrous clothing. This theme is common in Coptic literature, particularly in panegyrics to Michael.[125]

9. In Old Irish

Old Irish literature is replete with biblical legends, some of very ancient provenance. In his survey of this literature, Martin McNamara records a number of works that deal with Adam.[126]

1. *Saltair na Rann* ("The Psalter of the Quatrains"): St. John Seymour, studying the sacred history embodied in the 162 cantos of the tenth-century poem, *Saltair na Rann* concluded that cantos 6-11 make use both of Latin *Vita Adam et Evae* and of *Apocalypse of Moses*. This would mean a knowledge of *Apocalypse of Moses* in the West that is

---

[125] See Van Lanschoot, 1947, 260-268. On p. 265 in note 2 he gives a number of references to Coptic texts dealing with this legend. Texts of this character also exist in Greek manuscripts and the examination of Michael traditions in relationship to the Adam literature should be a major research topic in its own right. Denis, *Introduction (2nd ed. manuscript)*, points out some further Coptic usages of the the Adam books. The fragmentary text relating the encounter of Eve with the serpent, published by Giron, appears to have no connection with the Adam literature: see Giron, 1907, 23-25.

[126] McNamara, 1975. This work contains extensive bibliographical indications for the editions and translations of these works and should be consulted by the reader. We will not repeat material which he discusses. Many more details about *Saltair na Rann* may be found in Murdoch, 1973b, 146-177. A translation of the prose version of *Saltair na Rann*, found in the manuscript called *Lebor brec*, has been published by MacCarthy, 1892, 37-90.

otherwise unparalleled.[127] A recent study has been devoted by B. Murdoch to the Adam materials in the *Saltair na Rann*,[128] and many of its results have already been discussed above, in section 2. Murdoch stressed the antiquity of the Old Irish material in comparison with the continental and English analogues.[129] He further noted the primacy of *Saltair na Rann* vis-à-vis the rest of the Irish Adam works. It is his view that *Saltair na Rann* is based upon an otherwise unknown form of the *Vita Adam et Evae*, either of "a composite Latin document which contained both the Latin *Vita Adae et Evae* and the *Apocalypsis Mosis* or of a Latin version of the latter." Murdoch himself inclines in the direction of a modified form of the first hypothesis, though arguing that the role of *Apocalypse of Moses* material is less prominent that had been thought by some.[130] We may comment that such apparent "combinations" of material are exactly what is to be found in the Armenian *Penitence of Adam* and in the Georgian *Book of Adam*, which may be assumed to go back to Greek originals. It would be of interest to know the views of scholars of the Old Irish works now that those two documents have been published. An interesting further observation is that the Quest of Seth material lacks completely from the *Saltair na Rann* as well as the Holy Rood material that is sometimes associated with it.[131]

2. *Adam Octipartite*:[132] This also occurs in Latin,[133], in Slavonic,[134] and in a number of other languages. It was discussed above in con-

---

[127] Seymour, 1922, 121-133. He points out, for example, that in Canto 12 a herb called *ornamentum* (i.e. *odoramenta* or *odoramentum*) is mentioned, a detail not in Latin *Vita Adam et Evae* but occurring in *Apocalypse of Moses* (p. 130). On pages 132-133 he gives a small piece of otherwise unknown Irish apocryphal Adam literature, summarizing the Adam story.

[128] Murdoch, 1976.

[129] Murdoch, 1976, 29.

[130] Murdoch, 1976, 33-35; 1973b, 171-174.

[131] Murdoch, 1973b, 171-172 argues that there are reminiscences of this material in the *Saltair na Rann*.

[132] McNamara, 1975, 21-22. Details of the editions may be found in McNamara, 1975, 21. An English translation is Stokes, 1862, xl-xli (*non vidi*). The Irish material was surveyed by Förster, 1907-1908, 485.

nection with the Latin secondary Adam literature. Förster considers the ninth-century Latin text to be a translation of the Slavonic.[135]

3. A third text is *Poem on Adam's Head*, three verses on the composition of Adam's head.[136]

In a recent collection of Irish apocrypha in translation, the following works further relating to Adam have been translated:[137]

4. *The Creation of Adam:* This text open with the hours on which Adam was created, his composition from seven natural elements, and their significance. It is drawn from British Library Ms Egerton 1782, fol. 45.[138]

5. *Creation and Fall:* This is the text referred to by McNamara in his catalogue as "First Section of Biblical History: Creation, Fall of Lucifer, Adam and Eve."[139] He comments "This is a prose version of Cantos 4 through 9 of *Saltair na Rann* ... but has some additions and paraphrases from the larger Adam and Eve tradition that can be assumed to

---

[133] Förster, 1907-1908, 477; cf. Förster, 1921, 47-48.

[134] Stegmüller, 1950, no. 75.20, p. 34.

[135] McNamara, 1975, 22 discusses this document in some detail, including the traditions about Adam's creation from the four cardinal points. Förster's work is considered in some further detail in the next section, dealing with the Slavonic apocrypha. In his article, "Adam's Erschaffung und Namengebung," Max Förster gives preceding bibliography on the octipartite creation of Adam (Förster, 1907-08, 477-529, particularly on p. 483 and notes there). He published some additional information about the Latin and Irish texts in Förster, 1921, 47-48.

[136] McNamara, 1975, 23.

[137] Herbert and McNamara, 1990. I am particularly grateful to Dr. McNamara for encouragement in the writing of this section.

[138] Herbert and McNamara, 1990, 1 (translation), 163-164 (notes). See also Anderson, 1903, 243-253. Anderson published and translated the text from manuscript XL, Advocates Library, Edinburgh, fols. 45v-48v.

[139] McNamara, 1975, 16-17.

have been current."[140] Its sources are presumed to be the Latin *Vita Adam et Evae* and also *Apocalypse of Moses.*[141]

6. *The Penance of Adam:* According to McNamara this text occurs in at least two versions and its source is almost exclusively the *Vita Adam et Evae.* He notes that "In par. 5 there may be an influence from the *Apocalypsis Mosis* (29:13), not found in the *Vita,* in the angels and living creatures assembled around Adam."[142] The question of possible affinity of this text with the type underlying the Armenian *Penitence of Adam* and the Georgian *Book of Adam* should be investigated as was noted also for the previous work: see discussion of text, above.

7. *Adam and his Descendants:* This short poetic piece deals with the expulsion, and the story of Cain and Abel, including the curses laid upon Cain. It is an extract from a poem beginning *Athair caich coimsid nimi* and contains a number of intriguing traditions, that merit further investigation.[143]

10. In Slavonic

1. *Satanel Text:* H. Gaylord published a fragment of Adam literature, affiliated with the Adam books, which was interpolated into the Russian manuscripts of the Slavonic version of *3 Apocalypse of Baruch.*[144] This text was subsequently translated into German by R. Stichel who wrote a commentary and an introduction setting it into its context in Slavonic

---

140   Herbert and McNamara, 1990, 165.

141   Above, in the discussion of the *Saltair na Rann* we have considered the possible implications of this phenomenon.

142   Herbert and McNamara, 1990; the translation is found on pp. 8-11 and the notes cover pp. 165-166. The work is catalogued in McNamara, 1975, 18. Following *Penance of Adam,* Herbert and McNamara give, under the title "The Death of Adam," the portion of the *Saltair na Rann* dealing with Adam's death (1990, 12-17, and notes on 167). This again seems to show some dependance on the primary Adam writings.

143   Herbert and McNamara, 1990, translation on pp. 17-18 and notes on p. 167.

144   Gaylord, 1982, 303-309. On Satanel, see the extensive discussion in Turdeanu, 1981, 17-31

and Byzantine ecclesiastical literature. Stichel regards it as a translation from Greek, and makes an attempt at reconstruction of that Greek original.[145] This fragment deals with the deception of Eve by the serpent who was possessed by Satanael. This Slavonic text contains material additional to that included in the Slavonic *Vita Adam et Evae* and related to traditions of the penitence and fall of Satan.

2. *Creation of Adam:* F.A. Andersen published parts of a Slavonic text dealing with the creation of Adam, which he compared with the material on the creation of Adam in *2 Enoch.*[146]

3. *Creation Account:* Another Slavonic creation account is translated and discussed by Jagić.[147] This text contains interesting traditions, including that of the three trees planted by Adam. This text has connections, he claims, with the Latin *Vita Adam et Evae.*

4. *Adam Material in the Slavonic Palaeas:* Jagić also discusses the relationship between the Adam material in the two Slavonic *Palaeas* and the Slavonic *Vita Adam et Evae*, showing how much in the *Palaeas* is not included in the Slavonic *Vita Adam et Evae.*[148]

5. *Adam Octipartite:* One text Jagić gives in this connection is the Slavonic text parallel to the Irish *Adam Octipartite* referred to in the previous section. This had already been discussed at some length in an

---

[145]   Stichel, 1989, 116-128.

[146]   Andersen, n.d., 1-26; the text and notes may be found on pp. 17-25.

[147]   Jagić, 1893, 44-47. Stegmüller, 1950, 76.1-5 refers to a work *De Adami Compositione* which was edited in two Croatian-Glagolithic versions, and one Russian version. He reports that the Croatian-Glagolithic versions were both edited by Jagić, 1868 and [n.d.] The Russian version was published by Pypin, 1862, 12-14. We do not have sufficient information at our disposal to determine whether these are works referred to in Nos. 3 and / or 4 of this section or not. A corpus of translations of all these texts, and of the further rich materials referred to by Jagić 1893 is a clear and pressing *desideratum.*

[148]   Jagić, 1893, pp. 58-64.

article by Max Förster in 1907-08.[149] Förster edited a comparable Latin version from six Latin manuscripts. He argues that the Slavonic and Latin texts must go back to a Greek *Vorlage*. This text has been discussed by Turdeanu as is noted in section 12 below.[150]

11. In Medieval Hebrew

1. The *Sefer HaRazim*, according to some manuscripts, was revealed to Adam.[151]

2. *A Prayer of Adam:* A. Jellinek prints a number of texts relating to Noah, among which is a fragment entitled: זו תפילת אדם הראשון.[152] This is a prayer, attributed to Adam, at the time of the expulsion from the Garden of Eden, which is followed by a revelation, after three days, mediated by the angel Raziel. This text is drawn from a medieval composition known as *Sefer Raziel*, which is related to the *Sefer HaRazim*.[153]

2. *Repentance of Adam in Pirqe de R. Eliezer:* I. Lévi dealt with the tradition of Adam's repentance which is to be found in *Pirqe de R. Eliezer*. He finds no parallels to it and regards it as due to Christian influence.[154]

3. Some evidence for the circulation of a Jewish apocryphal tradition about the creation of Adam by angels has been discerned in an illumi-

---

[149]   Förster, 1907-08, 477-529. He refers to various Slavonic versions on p. 484.

[150]   Turdeanu, 1981, 418-435 discusses in some detail the tradition of this text in the Slavonic and Roumanian languages and its affiliations with *2 Enoch*.

[151]   Most readily available in Morgan, 1983.

[152]   Jellinek, 1938, 3.156-159. In Rabbinic tradition, it may be noted, Psalm 92 is attributed to Adam.

[153]   Jellinek, 1938, xxxii.

[154]   Lévi, 1889, 86-87. Charlesworth, 1981 quotes as relevant the article of Lieberman, 1962. This is a mistake by Charlesworth, for that article deals not with any Adamic literature, but with a halachic work entitled *Ḥayyē 'Adam*.

nation in the 14th century Haggadah called *Sister to the Golden Haggadah*.[155]

4. There are, it should be noted, extensive traditions about the protoplasts in Rabbinic literature. These are not set forth here, since they do not constitute "Books of Adam" properly understood.[156]

12. Other Medieval Adam Writings

There are numerous works in the eastern and western European vernaculars dealing with the life of Adam and Eve or various associated incidents. A number of them were referred to above, in the sections dealing with Latin, Slavonic and Old Irish writings and notes on some more follow in the present section.[157] A survey article of the texts relevant particularly to the study of the German material, but containing very much more, was published by Brian O. Murdoch.[158] We have not followed his analysis systematically, because our focus of interest is much broader. The result of that, however, is that our notes are rather episodic. They are in no way intended to be exhaustive, but merely to provide a brief indication of some the wealth of material available. In Murdoch's article and in the researches mentioned in this section the interested reader may find further bibliographical keys and guidance.

1. There are retellings of the Adam stories in Old and Middle High German poems of the eleventh and twelfth centuries, the most notable of which are the *Wiener Genesis*, the *Vorauer Genesis*, and the *Anegenge*.[159] A number of studies have been made of these including a substantial one by Brian Murdoch. His study of these works is chiefly from a theological-historical point of view, though it contains much of

---

155   Friedman, 1988, 1-7.

156   See, for example, the material assembled by Schäfer, 1986, 69-93, as well as older writings, such as Altmann, 1944-45, 371-391. Much material, of course, is assembled by Ginzberg, 1928, 6 volumes, and also by Schürer, 1977.

157   Murdoch, 1976, 30-31 gives many references.

158   Murdoch, 1973.

159   Murdoch, 1972.

interest as to their sources and character,[160] and he stresses the difficulty of isolating precisely the sources on which they drew.

2. The Middle High German poem on Adam and Eve by Lutwin has also been the object of a number of studies. Eis estimates it highly as a literary work, and he is neither the first nor the last to do so. Others, however, have denied Lutwin originality, pointing out his dependence on the Latin *Vita Adam et Evae*.[161] This poem includes the Holy Rood legend at the end.

3. The Anglo-Norman play, entitled *Ordo representacionis Adam* or *Le Jeu d'Adam* has received much attention. It contains, in addition to other material, scenes on the stories of Adam and Eve and Cain and Abel. Intriguingly, some of the elements of this play are intimately related to Romanesque sculptural programs.[162]

4. Migne cites a medieval French text, often reprinted, called *Vie de Nostre-Seigneur Jésu Christi* which tells the story of the quest of Seth, and he notes that it is one of many forms of this legend and extant in many copies.[163]

5. Above, in connection with the discussion of the Latin *Vita Adam et Evae,* one Middle English work was mentioned, the *Canticum de Creatione*. Another Middle English poem on the protoplasts has also been published from BM Add. 39574 by Day and a discussion of the affinities

---

160   Murdoch, 1972, 185-229 presents an extensive bibliography of ancient and medieval writings relating to the Fall or to the exegesis of Genesis 1-3.

161   Eis, 1935, 27 and further references there. He has an extensive introductory study to the poem in that volume, on pp. 25-106. The relationship between Lutwin's *Adam und Eva* and the Latin manuscripts of *Latin Vita Adam et Evae* was discussed by Dunstan, 1929. See also the two studies of this work by Halford, 1980 and 1984.

162   Noomen, 1971. Some more recent studies include Colletta, 1978, 73-82; Vaughan, 1983, 81-114; Justice, 1987, 851-64 with many references to earlier studies.

163   Migne, 1856-58, 1.387-390.

of the various Middle English poems may be found in her work.[164] A long discussion of early English stories of the fall of Lucifer, and of their relationship to Milton was published by Dustoor.[165] Malory's sources in *The Tale of the Sankgreal* for the story of the three spindles made from the branches of the tree of knowledge, are discussed extensively by Quinn.[166] The tree of the fall is the tree of salvation in this tradition, and the tree is made of three different woods. Both these elements occur in various Rood Tree stories.[167]

6. There exist dramas on the creation of the world and the protoplasts in Cornish and in Breton which form part of the medieval development of these themes. In the Breton play, for example, Seth not only goes to Paradise to search for the oil, but enters it and explores its parts.[168] The Breton drama also relates the fall of Lucibel and his followers and the change of his name to Lucifer, the naming of the animals, and the fall of Adam. The Cornish drama *The Beginning of The World* is also partly dependent on the *Vita Adam et Evae*, either directly or indirectly, and has reworked the plot in a number of ways.[169] There were a number of other later medieval reworkings of the Adam material, often in dramatic

---

[164]   Day, 1921. The text, which she entitles *The Life of Adam and Eve* is printed on pp. 76-99, while her introductory discussion may be found on pp. xxii-xxxii. On the Middle English material, see also section 2, above.

[165]   Dustoor, 1930, 213-267.

[166]   Quinn, 1965.

[167]   Hill, 1965, 203-222 points out the existence of two mid-15th century texts of Quest of Seth legend not discussed by Quinn 1963. She publishes the texts and discusses them in relation to the medieval Rood Tree material. See further, on this tradition, section 1 above.

[168]   Bernard, 1888, 151-153. In Bernard, 1889, 419-421 and 433-437 is the penitence story; unfortunately, I was unable to view the subsequent numbers of *Revue Celtique* which doubtless contain the rest of the story. The part I examined is clearly related to the Latin *Vita Adam et Evae*, though it has many individual elements in it.

[169]   Thus in lines 325ff. Adam asks for the oil of mercy and is refused it before his expulsion from Eden. The quest of Seth for the oil is also found at its proper place (733ff.). The play includes many other fascinating details: see Norris, 1859, vol. 1.

form. They are beyond the possible scope of our present work, though they contain much of interest.[170]

7. Turdeanu discusses "The Plaint of Adam" and "The Poem of Adam and Eve" which were developed in Byzantine religious poetry and have a rich continuation in Slavonic texts. In Roumanian religious folklore,[171] Adam's lament develops quite significantly. It should perhaps be noted that the Armenian *Repentance of Adam and Eve* also contains a lament of Adam and Eve.[172]

8. Turdeanu has also studied a popular Roumanian verse poem which includes a rich repertoire of elements drawn from the Adam literature.[173] It includes themes related to the *Adam Octipartite* traditions referred to above which entered Roumanian culture from Slavonic.[174]

9. A modern Greek oral retelling of the story of the cheirograph of Adam was recorded by G. Megas and set into relationship with the apocryphal material.[175]

These are but a few examples of the implications and developments of the Adam tales, as they were taken up in the literary traditions of east and west alike.

---

[170]   Brockman, 1974, 169-182 has written an interesting study showing how the writer of the Chester *Creation* has used to dramatic effectiveness the older exegetical and narrative traditions from late antique and earlier medieval times. Extensive material relating to the Adam texts is present in the fifteenth-century Coventry plays published by Block, 1922. This cycle includes the following plays, relevant to our theme: *The Creation of Heaven and the Angels, Fall of Lucifer, The Creation of the World and Man, Fall of Man, Cain and Abel,* and *Noah and the Death of Lamech.*

[171]   Turdeanu, 1981, 122-144.

[172]   Lipscomb, 1990, 229-230.

[173]   Turdeanu, 1981, 404-435.

[174]   See in sections dealing with secondary Adam literature in Latin, Old Irish and Slavonic.

[175]   Megas, 1928, 305-309. This was discussed above, in Chapter 1 section 3 and in section 1 and 6 of the present chapter.

Appendix

Note on Gnostic and Mandean Adam Texts

The Gnostic and Mandean Adam texts have been excluded from our survey, since they lead into quite other fields of enquiry. Here, however, we append a few indicative notes, without any claim at exhaustiveness or comprehensiveness.

The chief surviving Gnostic Adam work is *Apocalypse of Adam* from among the Coptic codices of Nag Hammadi (V, 5:64,1-85,32).[176] It seems to have been written originally in Greek, perhaps in the second century or later, and the surviving copy is of the fourth century C.E.[177] Both from its title and from its framework the book is clearly an apocalypse and it also bears testamentary features, being apparently a deathbed revelation to Seth. It probably comes from the Sethian Gnostic sect. It is relevant to the present study, at least to note the conclusions of Nickelsburg, who has discussed the relationship between this writing and the primary Adam writings. He says: "*Adam and Eve* 29:2-10 + 49-50 and the Gnostic *Apocalypse of Adam* ... derive from a testament of Adam that was influenced by traditions found in 1 Enoch, which are reflected in both *Adam and Eve* and *ApocAd.*"[178] Robinson maintains that this work has affinities "with the *Testament of Adam* and with the Jewish traditions about Adam and Seth cited by Josephus."[179]

---

[176]   The text was first published and translated in Böhlig, and Labib, 1963, pp. 86-117. Introductory comments are those of MacRae, 1976, 9-10.

[177]   There is a fairly extensive bibliography on *Apocalypse of Adam* in Charlesworth, 1981, 72-74 and 271-272 and in MacRae, 1976, 10. Compare also the material adduced by Nickelsburg, 1981, 515. A recent edition and translation with instructive introduction and commentary is Morard, 1985, while the study by Hedrick, 1980 should also be noted.

[178]   Nickelsburg, 1981, 525.

[179]   Robinson, 1982, 8. The gnosticizing tendencies attributed to various Adam books have been mentioned above. This point is reiterated by Bianchi, 1969, 6-13, and particularly pp. 9-12. There he deals with elements of the *Vita Adam et Evae* as well as of other Adam books. He emphasizes, among others, the idea of Adam's resemblance to God, and its general high evaluation of Adam. This feature he sees as underlying the Judaeo-

Epiphanius in *haer*. 26,8.1 refers to many Gnostic books attributed to Seth and "revelations" to Adam. It is not certain that he is referring to the *Apocalypse of Adam* which was mentioned above.[180] Adamic traditions of Gnostic character have supposedly been detected in *2 Enoch*, but this is far from certain.[181] Perhaps Gnostic and certainly heretical were the "teachings of Adam" attacked in the sixth century by the Egyptian bishop John of Parallos.[182]

Adam plays a central role in Mandean thought and many Mandean writings and traditions are related to him. In particular, the *Ginza*, a central book of the Mandeans, is attributed to Adam.[183]

---

which he deals include the role of the woman, Adam's knowledge, and the nature of evil.

[180] Denis, *Introduction (2nd ed. manuscript)* refers to some other possible citations of Adam works attributed to Gnostic sources.

[181] Guerin, 1968, 13-14. This is, of course, only one of numerous attempts to find Gnostic elements in various Adam writings and other apocryphal works. One of the better known ones is of Preuschen, *Adamschriften*, and there are others. With the emergence of the Nag Hammadi material, of course, much speculation of this sort can be tested against the reality of assuredly Gnostic texts.

[182] Morard, 1985, 9-10.

[183] On Adam in Mandean thought, see Drower, 1960. Certain Mandean works include the name of Adam in their titles; see Bibliography in *ibid*, 114-115. Compare also the comments of Frey, 1928, 134 and Stegmüller, 1950, 74.35-40. Fabricius, as reported above in Chapter 2, also refers to the Mandean material on Adam. The first translation of the *Ginza* was published as part of the Adamic apocrypha by Migne, 1856-58, 1,1-284; see further *ibid* 283-285.

BIBLIOGRAPHY AND BIBLIOGRAPHICAL ABBREVIATIONS

In the book, all works are referred to by author and date, as listed in this bibliography.

ADLER, W.
1989   *Time Immemorial: Archaic History and Its Sources in Christian Chronography from Julius Africanus to George Syncellus.* Dumbarton Oaks Studies, 26. Washington, Dumbarton Oaks.

ALEXANDRE, M.
1988   *Le commencement du Livre Genèse I-V: La version grecque de la Septante et sa réception.* Paris, Beauchesne.

ALTMANN, A.
1944-45   "The Gnostic Background of the Rabbinic Adam Legends." *Jewish Quarterly Review.* NS 35: 371-391.

ANASYAN, H.S.
1959   Հայկական Մատենագիտություն (*Armenian Bibliology*). vol. 1. Erevan, Academy of Sciences.

ANDERSEN, F. A.
n.d.   "On Reading Genesis 1-3." *Interchange.* 33: 1-26.

ANDERSON, A.O.
1903   "Pennaid Adaim." *Revue Celtique.* 26: 243-253.

ANDERSON, G.
1989   "Celibacy or Consummation in the Garden: Reflections on Early Jewish and Christian Interpretations of the Garden of Eden." *Harvard Theological Review.* 82: 121-48.

ANDREWS, H.T.
1964   *An Introduction to the Apocryphal Books of the Old Testament.* Grand Rapids, Michigan, Baker Book House.

APTOWITZER, V.
1922   *Kain und Abel in der Agada, den Apokryphen, der hellenistischen, christlichen und mohammedanischen Literatur.* Vienna and Leipzig, Löwt.

1924   "Les éléments juifs dans la légende du Golgotha." *Revue des Etudes Juives.* 79: 145-162.

ASSEMANUS, G.S.
1719-1728   *Bibliotheca Orientalis.* Rome.

AVALICHVILI, Z.
1927-28   "Notice sur une version géorgienne de la Caverne des Trésors." *Revue de l'Orient Chrétien.* 26: 381-405.

1927-28   "Appendice." *Revue de l'Orient Chrétien.* 26: 402-405.

BAGATTI, B.
1980   "Una Nota sul *Combattimento di Adamo.*" *Henoch.* 2: 58-62.

BAMBERGER, B.J.
1962   "Adam, Books of." *Interpreter's Dictionary of the Bible.* Nashville and New York, Abingdon, 1: 44-45.

BAMBERGER, J.
1901   *Die Literatur der Adambücher und die haggadischen Elemente in der syrischen Schatzhöhle.* Aschaffenburg, C. Krebs.

BATTIFOL, P.
1895   "Apocalypses Apocryphes II, Apocalypses chrétiens." *Dictionnaire de la Bible.* Paris, Letouzey et Ané, 1: 764-765.

BATTISTA, A. AND B. BAGATTI
1980   *La Caverna dei Tresori.* Studium Biblicum Franciscanum, Collectio Minor 26. Jerusalem, Franciscan
Printing Press.

1982   *Il Combattimento di Adamo. Testo arabo inedito
con traduzione italiana e commento.* Studium
Biblicum Franciscanum. Collectio Minor, 29. vol.
1982. Jerusalem, Franciscan Printing Press.

BAUMSTARK, A.
1922   *Geschichte der syrischen Literatur mit Ausschluß
der christlich-palästinenischen Texte.* Bonn,
Marcus und Weber.

BEER, G.
1905   "Pseudepigraphen des Alten Testaments 39. Die
Adambücher." *Realencyclopädie für protes-
tantische Theologie und Kirche.* 3 ed. Leipzig,
Hinrichs, 16: 263-264.

BERNARD, E.
1888   "La création du monde, mystère breton." *Revue
Celtique.* 9: 149-207; 322-353.

1889   "La création du monde, mystère breton." *Revue
Celtique.* 10: 192-211, 414-455.

BERTRAND, D. A.
1985   "Le destin 'post mortem' des protoplastes selon la
'Vie grecque d'Adam et Eve'." *La Littérature
intertestamentaire: Colloque de Strasbourg (17-19
Octobre 1983).* ed. A. Caquot. Paris, Presses
universitaires de France, 109-118.

1987a   *La vie grecque d'Adam et Eve.* Recherches intertestamentaires 1. Paris, Maisonneuve.

1987b   La vie greque d'Adam et d'Eve." *La Bible: Ecrits
intertestamentaires.* ed. A. Dupont-Sommer and M.
Philonenko. Paris, Gallimard, 1767-1796.

BEZOLD, C.
1888   Die Schatzhöhle, syrisch und deutsch heraus-
            gegeben. Leipzig, Hinrichs.

1906   "Das arabisch-äthiopische Testamentum Adami."
            Orientalische Studien Theodor Nöldeke zum
            siebzigsten Geburtstag gewidmet. Giessen,
            Töpelmann, 893-912.

BIANCHI, U.
1969   "Gnostizismus und Anthropologie." Kairos. 11: 6-13.

1971   "La rédemption dans les livres d'Adam." Numen.
            18: 1-8.

BLAKE, R.P.
1925   "Georgian Theological Literature." Journal of
            Theological Studies. 26: 50-64.

BLOCK, K. S.
1922   Ludus Coventriae, or the Plaie called Corpus Christi.
            Early English Text Society Extra Series, 120. London,
            Oxford University Press.

BÖHLIG, A. AND P. LABIB
1963   Koptisch-gnostische Apokalypsen aus Codex V von
            Nag Hammadi im Koptischen Museum zu Alt-
            Kairo. Wissenschaftliche Zeitschrift der Martin-
            Luther-Universität. Halle-Wittenberg.

BOLL, F.
1908   "Appendix." Catalogus Codicum Astrologorum
            Graecorum. Brussels, 174-181.

BOWMAN, J.
1981-82   "The Malef." Abr-Nahrain. 20: 1-19.

BROCK, S.P.
1974   "A Syriac Life of Abel." Le Muséon. 87: 467-492.

1979   "Jewish Traditions in Syriac Sources." Journal of
            Jewish Studies. 30: 212-232.

1982   "Clothing Metaphors as a Means of Theological Expression in Syriac Tradition." *Typus, Symbol, Allegorie bei den östlichen Vätern und ihren Parallelen im Mittelalter.* ed. M. Schmidt in collaboration with C.F. Geyer. Regensburg, Friederich Pustet, 11-38.

BROCKMAN, B.A.
1974   "Cain and Abel in the Chester *Creation.*" *Medievalia et Humanistica.* ed. P. M. Clogan. Denton, TX, North Texas State University, NS 5: 169-182.

BUDGE, E.A.W.
1886   *The Book of the Bee.* Anecdota Oxoniensa, Semitic Series 1.2. Oxford, Oxford University Press.

1914   *Coptic Martyrdoms etc. in the Dialect of Upper Egypt.* London, British Museum.

1927   *The Book of the Cave of Treasures.* London, Religious Tract Society.

BURMESTER, O.H.E.
1938   "Egyptian Mythology in the Coptic Apocrypha." *Orientalia.* NS 7: 355-367.

1975   *Koptische Handschriften 1: Handschriften fragmente der Staats- und Universitäts Bibliothek Hamburg.* Verzeichnis der orientalischen Handschriften in Deutschland. vol. 21, 1. Wiesbaden, Frans Steiner Verlag.

CARDONA, G.
1967   "Sur le gnosticisme en Arménie: les livres d'Adam." *Le origini dello gnosticismo.* ed. U. Bianci. Leiden, Brill, 645-648.

CERIANI, A.M.
1868   *Monumenta sacra et profana, t. 5, Opuscula et fragmenta miscella magnam partem apocrypha.* Milan, Biblioteca Ambrosiana.

CHACHANOV, A.
1894   "Памятники грузинской отреченной литературы (Monuments of Georgian Monastic Literature)." Журнал Министерства народного просвещения (*Journal of the Ministry of Education*). 296: 35-49.

1895   "Очерки по истории грузинской словесности (Studies in History of the Georgian Philology)." Чтения в императорском обществе истории и древностей российских "Изгнание Адама из рая, Нимрод и семь послепотопных народов, книга Нимрода (The Expulsion of Adam from Paradise, Nimrod and the Seven Post-diluvial Peoples, The Book of Nimrod)." Сборник материалов для описания местностей и племен Кавказа. (*Collection of Materials for the Description of the Areas and Peoples of the Caucasus*). 26: 19-44.

CHARLES, R.H.,
1913   *The Apocrypha and Pseudepigrapha of the Old Testament.* 1913, Oxford: Oxford University Press.

CHARLESWORTH, J. H.
1979   "A History of Pseudepigrapha Research: The Re-emerging Importance of the Pseudepigrapha." *ANRW* 19.2. ed. W. H. a. H. Temporini.   Berlin & New York, de Gruyter, 77-81.

1981   *The Pseudepigrapha and Modern Research with a Supplement.* Septuagint and Cognate Studies, 7s. 2 ed. Chico CA, Scholars Press.

1983, 1985   Charlesworth, J.H., ed. *The Old Testament Pseudepigrapha.* , Doubleday: Garden City, NY.

CLARK, K. W.
1952   *Checklist of Manuscripts in St. Catherine's Monastery, Mount Sinai.* Washington, Library of Congress.

COLLETTA, J. P.
    1978   "Influence of the Visual Arts evident in the Jeu d'Adam." *Studies in Medieval Culture*. ed. John R. Sommerfeldt and Thomas H. Seiler. Medieval Institute, Western Michigan University, 12: 73-82.

CONYBEARE, F. C.
    1894-95   "On the Apocalypse of Moses." *Jewish Quarterly Review*. 7: 216-235.

COUSIN, H.
    1974   "Sépulture criminelle et sépulture prophétique." *Revue Biblique*. 81: 384-386.

COWLEY, R. W.
    1988   *Ethiopian Biblical Commentary: A Study in Exegetical Tradition and Hermeneutics*. Cambridge, Cambridge University Press.

COWLEY, R. AND F. A. TEFERU
    1971   "The Study of Geez Manuscripts in Tégre Province." *Journal of Ethiopian Studies*. 9 (1): 21-25.

CRUM, W. E.
    1909   *Catalogue of Coptic Manuscripts in the Collection of the John Rylands Library*. Manchester, Manchester University Press.

DAY, M.
    1921   *The Wheatley Manuscript*. Early English Text Society Original Series, 155. London, Humphrey Milford, Oxford University Press.

DENIS, A. -.M.
    1970   *Introduction aux pseudépigraphes grecs d'Ancien Testament*. Leiden, Brill.

    1987   *Concordance grecque des pseudépigraphes d'Ancien Testament: concordance, corpus des textes, indices*. Louvain-la-Neuve, Université catholique de Louvain.

DILLMANN, A.
1853   "Das christliche Adambuch des Morgenlandes aus dem Äthiopischen mit Bemerkungen übersetzt." *Jahrbücher des bibl. Wissenschaft*, 5. Göttingen, 1-144 (*non vidi*).

1858   "Bericht über das äthiopische Buch clementinischer Schriften." *Nachrichten von der Gesellschaft der Wissenschaften zu Göttingen.* 17-19: 185-226.

DINDORF, W.
1829   *Georgius Syncellus et Nicephorus CP.* Bonn.

DOBSCHÜTZ, E. V.
1912   *Das Decretum Gelasianum.* Texte und Untersuchungen zur Geschichte der altchristlichen Literature, 38.4: 1912. Leipzig, Hinrichs.

DROWER, E. S.
1960   *The Secret Adam: A Study of Naṣorean Gnosis.* Oxford, Oxford University Press.

DUNSTAN, A. C.
1929   "The Middle High German 'Adam und Eva' by Lutwin and the Latin 'Vita Adae et Evae'." *Modern Language Review.* 24: 191-99.

1931   "The Middle English Canticum de Creatione and the LatinVita Adae et Evae." *Anglia.* 55: 431-442.

DUSTOOR, P. E.
1930   "Legends of Lucifer in Early English and in Milton." *Anglia: Zeitschrift für englische Philologie.* 54: 213-267.

DŽANAŠVILI, M.
1909   "Изгнание Адама из рая, Нимрод и семь послепотопных народов, Книга Нимрода, Изгнание Адама из рая, Нимрод и семь послепотопных народов, книга Нимрода (The Expulsion of Adam from Paradise, Nimrod and the Seven Post-diluvial Peoples, The Book of Nimrod)." Сборник Материалов Дляа описаниыа месностеи и племен

Кавказа Сборник материалов для описания
местностей и племен Кавказа. (*Collection of
Materials for the Description of the Areas and
Peoples of the Caucasus*). 26: 19-44.

DŽAVACHOV, I.
1905   "Государственный строй древней Грузии и
древней Армении. " Издания факультета
восточных языков (The State Structure of Ancient
Georgia and Ancient Armenia). Имп. С.-Петерсб.
Унив. Нр. 5; Тексты и разыскания по армяно-
грузинской филологии, кн. 8. (*Publications of
the Faculty of Oriental Languages of St.
Petersburg, 5, Texts and Studies in Armenian and
Georgian Philology, 8*). St. Petersburg.

EGANYAN, O., A. ZEYT'UNYAN AND P. ANT'ABYAN
1965   Ցուցակ Ձեռագրաց Մաշտոցի Անվան Մատենադարանի
(*Catalogue of Manuscripts of the Maštoc'
Matenadaran*). vol. 1. Erevan, Academy of
Sciences.

EIS, G.
1935   *Beiträge zur mittelhochdeutschen Legende und
Mystik: Untersuchungen und Texte*. Germanische
Studien, 161. reprint. Berlin, Kraus.

EISSFELDT, O.
1965   *The Old Testament: An Introduction*. Oxford,
Blackwell.

EVANS, J.M.
1966   "Microcosmic Adam." *Medium Aevum*. 35: 38-42.

1968   *Paradise Lost and the Genesis Traditions*. Oxford,
Clarendon Press.

FABRICIUS, J.A.
1713   *Codex Pseudepigraphus Veteris Testamenti*.
Hamburg and Leipzig, Liebezeit.

1723   *Codicis Pseudepigraphi Veteris Testamenti Volumen*
              Alterum accedit Josephi veteris Christiani auctoria
              Hypomnesticon. Hamburg, Felginer.

FERNANDEZ MARCOS, N.
1983   "Vida de Adan y Eva (Apocalipsis de Moises)."
              Apocrifos del Antiquo Testamento. ed. A. Diez
              Macho. Madrid, Ediciones Cristiandad, 2: 316-352.

FLUSSER, D.
1971   "Palaea Historica - An Unknown Source of Biblical
              Legends." *Essays in Aggadah and Folk-Literature.*
              Jerusalem, Magnes, 48-79.

FÖRSTER, M.
1907-08   "Adam's Erschaffung und Namengebung: Ein
              lateinisches Fragment des s.g. slawischen Henoch."
              Archiv für Religionswissenschaft. 11: 477-529.

1910   "Das älteste mittellateinische Gesprächbüchlein."
              Romanische Forschungen. 27: 342-348.

1921   "Die mittelirische Version von Adams Erschaffung."
              Zeitschrift für celtische Philologie. 13: 47-48.

FORSYTH, N.
1987   *The Old Enemy: Satan and the Combat Myth.*
              Princeton, Princeton University Press.

FREY, J.B.
1928   "Adam (Livres apocryphes sous son nom)."
              Dictionnaire de la Bible, Supplements. ed. L. Pirot
              et al. Paris, Letouzey et Ané, 1: cols. 101-34.

FRIEDMAN, M.
1988   "A Jewish Motif of the Creation of Man." *Pro-*
              ceedings of the Ninth World Congress of Jewish
              Studies. ed. M. Friedmann *et alii.* Jerusalem, 1-7.

FUCHS, C.
1900   "Das Leben Adams und Evas." *Die Apokryphen und*
              Pseudepigraphen des Alten Testaments, Band 2, Die

Pseudepigraphen. ed. E. Kautzsch. Tübingen, Mohr, 506-528.

GAULMYN, G.
1615   "Notes on Michael Psellus, *De Daemonum Operatione*" *PG.* 122: 853-854.

GAYLORD, H.E.
1982   "How Satanael lost his '-el'." *Journal of Jewish Studies.* 33: 303-309.

GELZER, H.
1885   *Sextus Julius Africanus und die byzantinische Chronographie.* Leipzig; Hinrichs. repr. N.Y. 1967.

GERÖ, S.
1980   "The Legend of the Fourth Son of Noah." *Harvard Theological Review.* 73: 321-330.

GIBSON, M.D.
1901   *Kitāb al-Māgall or The Book of the Rolls, One of the Books of Clement.* Studia Sinaitica, 8. Apocrypha Arabica. London, Cambridge University Press.

GINZBERG, L.
1901   "Adam, Book of." *The Jewish Encyclopedia.* New York and London, Funk and Wagnalls, 1: 179-180.

1928   *The Legends of the Jews.* 6 vols. Philadelphia, Jewish Publication Society.

GIRON, N.
1907   *Légendes coptes: Fragments inédits.* Paris, Geuthner.

GOODENOUGH, E.R.
1958   "A Jewish-Gnostic Amulet of the Roman Period." *Greek, Roman and Byzantine Studies.* 1: 71-80.

GÖTZE, A.
1922   "Die Schatzhöhle: Überlieferung und Quellen." *Sitzungsberichte der Heidelberger Akademie der Wissenschaften: Philos.-Hist. Klasse.* 4: 1-92.

1923   "Die Nachwirking der Schatzhöhle." *Zeitschrift für Semitistik und verwandte Gebiete.* 2: 51-94.

1924   "Die Nachwirking der Schatzhöhle." *Zeitschrift für Semitistik und verwandte Gebiete.* 3: 53-71.

GRAF, G.

1944   *Geschichte der christlichen arabischen Literatur: Erster Band, Die Übersetzungen.* Studi e Testi, 118. vol. 1. Vatican, Biblioteca Apostolica Vaticana.

GRÉBAUT, S.

1911   "Littérature éthiopienne pseudo-clémentine." *Revue de l'Orient Chrétien.* 16 (6): 73.

1913   "Le sixième jour de l'hexaméron d'Epiphane de Chypre." *Revue de l'Orient Chrétien.* 18 (8): 432-441.

1914   "Les Manuscrits éthiopiens de M. É. Delorme." *Revue de l'Orient Chrétien.* 19 (9): 17-23.

GUERIN, G.-A.

1968   "En marge de la légende d'Adam." *Bulletin du cercle Ernest-Renan.* 142: 13-14.

HAFFNER, A.

1921-22   "Das Hexaëmeron des Pseudo-Epiphanius." *Oriens Christianus.* 10-11: 91-145.

HALFORD, M.B.

1980   *Illustration and Text in Lutwin's Eva und Adam.* Göppinger Arbeiten zur Germanistik, 305. Göppingen, Kümmerle Verlag.

1981   "The Apocryphal Vita Adae et Evae: Some Comments on the Manuscript Tradition." *Neuphilologische Mitteilungen.* 82: 417-427.

1984   *Lutwin's Eva und Adam.* Göppinger Arteiten zur Germanistik, 401. Göppingen, Kümmerle Verlag.

HARL, M.
1962 "Adam et les deux arbres du Paradis (Gen. II-III) ou l'homme entre deux termes (μέσος - μετηόριος) chez Philon d'Alexandrie, pour une histoire de la doctrine du libre-arbitre." *Revue des Sciences Religieuses.* 50: 321-388.

1966 "La prise de conscience de la 'nudité' d'Adam: une interprétation de Genèse 3,7 chez les Pères grecs." *Studia Patristica* 7.1. Berlin, 486-495.

HARTOM, A.S.
1965 כרך א. אדם וחוה, צוואת בני יעקוב, צוואת משה. הספרים החיצונים סיפורי אגדה . Tel-Aviv, Yavneh.

HATCH, E. AND H.A. REDPATH
1954 *A Concordance to the Septuagint.* reprint. Graz, Akademische Verlag.

HEDRICK, C. W.
1980 *The Apocalypse of Adam: A Literary and Source Analysis.* SBLDS, 46. Chico, CA, Scholars.

HENRICHS, A. AND L. KOENEN
1975 "Die kölner Mani-Kodex (P.Colon. inv.nr. 4780 Περὶ τῆς γέννης τοῦ σώματος αὐτοῦ.) Edition der Seiten 1-72." *Zeitschrift für Papyrologie und Epigraphik.* 19 (1): 1-85.

HERBERT, M. AND M. MCNAMARA
1990 *Irish Biblical Apocrypha.* Edinburgh, T. & T. Clark.

HILL, B.
1965 "The Fifteenth-century Prose *Legend of the Cross before Christ.*" *Medium Aevum.* 34: 203-222.

HORSTMANN, C.
1878 *Sammlung Altenglischer Legenden.* Heilbronn, Henninger.

ISSAVERDENS, J.
1901   *The Uncanonical Writings of the O.T. found in the*
                Armenian Mss. of the Library of St. Lazarus.
                Venice, Mechitarist.

IVANOV, J.
1976   *Livres et Légendes Bogomiles (Aux Sources du*
                Catharisme). Paris, Maisonneuve et Larose.

JACIMIRSKIJ, A.I.
1921   Библиографический обзор апокрифов в
                южнославянской и русской письменности
                (*Bibliographical Survey of Apocrypha in South*
                Slavic and in Russian Languages). Petrograd.

JAGIČ, V.
[n.d.]   "De Adami compositione," in *Archiv za povjestnicu*
                jugoslavensku edited by K. Kukuljevic-Sakcinski, vol.
                9, pp. 105-108. (*non vidi*)

1868   "De Adami compositione." in *Prilozi k historiji*
                knjizevnosti naroda hrvatskoga i srbskoga. Zagreb,
                41-44.

1893   "Slavische Beiträge zu den biblischen Apocryphen,
                I, Die altkirchenslavischen Texte des Adamsbuche."
                Denkschr. kaiserl. Akademie der Wissenschaften,
                philos.-hist. Classe. Vienna, 42: 1-104.

JAMES, M.R.
1893   "A Fragment of the Apocalypse of Adam in Greek."
                Apocrypha Anecdota: A Collection of Thirteen
                Apocryphal Books and Fragments. Texts and
                Studies, 2. Cambridge, Cambridge University Press,
                138-145.

1920   *The Lost Apocrypha of the Old Testament: Their*
                Titles and Fragments. London, SPCK.

JAUBERT, A.
1971   *Clément de Rome, Epître aux Corinthiens.* Sources
                chrétiennes, 167;. Paris, Editions du Cerf.

JELLINEK, A.
1938   *Bet Ha-Midrasch.* reprint. Jerusalem, Bamberger and Wahrmann.

JOHNSON, M.D.
1985   "Life of Adam and Eve." *The Old Testament Pseudepigrapha.* ed. J. H. Charlesworth. Garden City, Doubleday, 2: 249-295.

JUSTICE, S.
1987   "The Authority of Ritual in the *Jeu d'Adam.*" *Speculum.* 62 (4): 851-864.

KABISCH, R.
1905   "Die Entstehungszeit der Apokalypse Mose." *Zeitschrift für die neutestamentliche Wissenschaft.* 6: 109-134.

KAHANA, A.
1956   הספרים החיצונים. Tel-Aviv, Masada, 1: [1]-[18]

KAUFMANN, J.
1932   "Adambuch." *Encyclopedia Judaica.* Berlin, Eschkol, 1. 788-792.

KLIJN, A.F.J.
1977   *Seth in Jewish, Christian and Gnostic Literature.* SNT, 46. Leiden, Brill.

KMOSKO, M.
1907   "Testamentum Patris Nostri Adam." *Patrologia Syriaca.* ed. R. Graffin. Paris, Firmin-Didot, 2: 1309-60, 1393-1410.

KOLENKOW, A.B.
1977   "Trips to the Other World in Antiquity and the Story of Seth in the Life of Adam and Eve." *SBL 1977 Seminar Papers.* ed. P.J. Achtemeier. Missoula, Scholars Press, 1-11.

KOROL, D.

1979   "Zum Bild der Vertreibung Adams und Evas in der neuen Katakombe an die via Latina und zur anthropomorphischen Darstellung Gottvaters." *Jahrbuch für Antike und Christentum.* 22: 175-190, plates 7-9.

KRONHOLM, T.
1978   *Motifs from Genesis 1-11 in the Genuine Hymns of Ephrem the Syrian with Particular Reference to the Influence of Jewish Exegetical Tradition.* Coniectanea Biblica Old Testament Series, 11. Lund, Gleerup.

K'URC'IKIDZE, C.
1964   "Adamis Apokrip'uli C'xovrebis K'art'uli Versia." *P'ilologiuri Dziebani.* 1: 97-136.

LACHS, S.T.
1982   "Some Textual Observations on the *Apocalypsis Mosis* and the *Vita Adae et Evae.*" *Journal for the Study of Judaism.* 13: 172-176.

LANTSCHOOT, A. VAN
1947   "Un Texte palimpseste de vat. copte 65." *Le Muséon.* 60: 260-268.

LASSALLE, V.
1974   "Deux reliefs romans inédits représentant des scènes de l'histoire d'Adam et Eve." *Hommage à André Dupont: Études médiévales languedociennes.* Montpellier, 185-192.

LEIPOLDT, J.
1904   *Ägyptische Urkunden aus den königlichen Museen zu Berlin: Koptische Urkunden.* vol. 1. Berlin, Weidmannsche Buchhandlung.

LÉVI, I.
1889   "Éléments chrétiens dans le Pirke de Rabbi Eliézer." *Revue des Etudes Juives.* 10: 86-87.

LEVISON, J.R.
1988   *Portraits of Adam in Early Judaism.* JSP Supplement Series 1. Sheffield, Sheffield Academic Press.

LIDDELL, H.G., R. SCOTT, & H.S. JONES
1961   *A Greek-English Lexicon.* Oxford: Oxford University Press.

LIEBERMANN, S.
1962   "בעל יחיי אדם׳ והגר״א מוילנא" *Kirjath Sepher.* 37: 413-414.

1972   "זניחין" *Tarbiẓ.* 62: 42-54.

LIECHTENHAN, R. VON
1902   "Die pseudepigraphe Literatur der Gnostiker." *Zeitschrift für die neutestamentliche Wissenschaft.* 3: 222-237.

LIPSCOMB, W. L.
1990   *The Armenian Apocryphal Adam Literature.* University of Pennsylvania Armenian Texts and Studies, 8. ed. M. E. Stone. Atlanta, Scholars Press.

LÜDTKE, W.
1911   "Beiträge zu slavischen Apokryphen, 5, Zum sogen. Index des Anastasios." *Zeitschrift für die alttestamentliche Wissenschaft.* 31: 230-235.

1919-20   "Georgische Adam-Bücher." *Zeitschrift für die alttestamentliche Wissenschaft* 38: 155-168.

MACCARTHY, B.
1892   *The Codex Palatino-Vaticanus No. 830.* Dublin.

MACRAE, G.
1976   "Adam, Apocalypse of," *Interpreters Dictionary of the Bible, Supplement Volume.* Nashville, Abingdon, 9-10.

MAGUIRE, H.
1987   "Adam and the Animals: Allegory and the Literal Sense in Early Christian Art." *Dumbarton Oaks Papers.* 41: 363-373.

MAHÉ, J. -P.
1981   "Le Livre d'Adam géorgien." *Studies in Gnosticism and Hellenistic Religions.* ed. R. van den Broek and M. J. Vermaseren. Leiden, Brill, 227-260.

1983   "Notes philologiques sur la version géorgienne de la *Vita Adae.*" *Bedi Kartlisa.* 41: 51-65.

MALAN, S.C.
1882   *The Book of Adam and Eve, also called The Conflict of Adam and Eve with Satan.* London, Williams and Norgate.

MARR, N.
1890-91   Article on Armenian Book of Adam, *Transactions of the Eastern Section of the Russian Imperial Archaeological Society.* 5, 6 (*non vidi*).

MARSHALL, F.H.
1925   *Old Testament Legends From a Greek Poem on Genesis and Exodus by Georgios Chumnos.* Cambridge, Cambridge University Press.

MAYSER, E.
1926   *Grammatik der griechischen Papyri aus der Ptolemäerzeit.* Berlin and Leipzig, de Gruyter.

MCNALLY, R.E.
1959   *The Bible in the Early Middle Ages.* Westminster MD, Newman Press.

MCNAMARA, M.
1975   *The Apocrypha in the Irish Church.* Dublin, Dublin Institute for Advanced Studies.

MEGAS, G.
       1928   "Das χειρόγραφον Adams. Ein Beitrag zu Col. 2:13-
                       15." *Zeitschrift für die neutestamentliche
                       Wissenschaft.* 27: 305-320.

MEYER, W.
       1878   "Vita Adae et Evae." *Abhandlungen der
                       königlichen Bayerischen Akademie der
                       Wissenschaften, Philosoph.-philologische Klasse.*
                       Munich: 14.3: 185-250.

MIGNE, J. -P.
       1856-58   *Dictionnaire des Apocryphes ou Collection de tous
                       les livres apocryphes relatifs à l'ancien et au
                       nouveau testament.* Troisième et dernière
                       Encyclopédie théologique, 23-24. Paris, Migne-
                       Ateliers catholiques.

MORARD, F.
       1985   *L'Apocalypse d'Adam.* Bibliothèque copte de Nag
                       Hammadi, Textes, 15. Quebec, Les Presses de
                       l'Université Laval.

MORGAN, M.A.
       1983   *Sepher Harazim: The Book of Mysteries.* Texts and
                       Translations 25, Pseudepigrapha Series 11. Chico
                       CA, Scholars Press.

MOSSHAMMER, A.A.
       1984   (ed.), *Georgius Syncellus, Ecloga Chronographica.*
                       Leipzig: Teubner.

MOZLEY, J.H.
       1929   "The Vitae Adae." *Journal of Theological Studies.*
                       30: 121-49.

       1930   "A New Text of the Story of the Cross." *Journal of
                       Theological Studies.* 31: 113-127.

MURDOCH, B.O.

1967 "The Garments of Paradise: A Note on the Wiener Genesis and the Anegenge." *Euphorion.* 61 (4): 375-382.

1972 *The Fall of Man in the Early Middle High German Biblical Epic: The 'Wiener Genesis', the 'Vorauer Genesis' and the 'Anegenge'.* Göppinger Arbeiten zur Germanistik, 58. Göppinger, Kümmerle Verlag.

1973a "Das deutsche Adambuch und die Adamlegenden des Mittelalters." *Deutsche Literatur des späten Mittelalters: Hamburger Colloquium 1973.* ed. W. Harms and L.P. Johnson. Hamburg, Erich Schmidt Verlag.

1973b "An Early Irish Adam and Eve: Saltair na Rann and the Traditions of the Fall." *Mediaeval Studies.* 35: 146-177.

1976 *The Irish Adam and Eve Story from Saltair na Rann: Volume 2, Commentary.* Dublin, Dublin Institute for Advanced Studies.

NAGEL, M.

1974 *La Vie grecque d'Adam et d'Eve.* Ph. D. dissertation, Strassbourg.

NAU, F.

1907 "Apotelesmata Apollonii Tyanensis." *Patrologia Syriaca.* ed. R. Graffin. Paris, Firmin-Didot, 2: 1363-85.

1908 "Clémentins (apocryphes)." *Dictionnaire de Théologie catholique.* 3: 216-219.

NEUMARK, D.

1910 *Geschichte der jüdischen Philosophie des Mittelalters.* vol. 1. Berlin, Reimer.

NICKELSBURG, G.W.E.

1981 "Some Related Traditions in the *Apocalypse of Adam,* the *Books of Adam and Eve,* and *1 Enoch.*"

The Rediscovery of Gnosticism. ed. B. Layton. Leiden, Brill, 2: 515-539.

1984 "The Bible Rewritten and Expanded: The Books of Adam and Eve." *Jewish Writings of the Second Temple Period.* ed. M. E. Stone. Philadelphia and Assen, Fortress and van Gorcum, 110-118.

NIDITCH, S.
1983 "The Cosmic Adam: Man as Mediator in Rabbinic Literature." *Journal of Jewish Studies.* 34: 137-146.

NOOMEN, W.
1971 *Le Jeu d'Adam (ordo representacionis Ade).* Les classiques français du Moyen Age 99. Paris.

NORDHEIM, E. VON
1980 *Die Lehre der Alten: 1 Das Testament als Literaturgattung im Judentum der hellenistisch-römischen Zeit.* Leiden, Brill.

NORRIS, E.
1859 *The Ancient Cornish Drama.* vol. 1. Oxford, Oxford University Press.

NOVAKOVIC, S.
1889 Примеры книжности и языка старого сербско-словенского (*Samples of Literature and Language of Ancient Serbo-Slavic*). Belgrade.

PIATELLI, E.
1968-69 "'Vita Adae et Evae'." *Annuario di Studi Ebraici.* 1: 9-23.

POIRIER, P.-H.
1983 "Fragments d'une version copte de la *Caverne de Trésors.*" *Orientalia.* 52: 415-423.

PORFIR'EV, I.
1872 Апокрифические сказания о ветхозаветных лицах и событиях (*Apocryphal Legends on Old-Testamental Personalities and Events*). Kazan, 1.76.

PREUSCHEN, E.
1900   "Die apokryphen gnostischen Adamschriften, aus
        dem Armenischen übersetzt und untersucht."
        Festgruss B. Stade. Giessen: Ricker, 163-252.

PUECH, E.
1988   Review of Bertrand, D.A., *La vie grecque d'Adam et
        Eve* (1987). *Revue Biblique*. 85: 584-585.

PYPIN, A.
1862   "Ложныеа и отреченные книги русской
        старины (False and Rejected Books of Russian
        Antiquity)." Памятники старинной русской
        литературы, 3. ed. Graf Kuseljev-Bezborodko. St.
        Petersburg.

QUINN, E.C.
1962   *The Quest of Seth for the Oil of Life*. Chicago,
        University of Chicago.

1965   "The Quest of Seth, Solomon's Ship and the Grail."
        Traditio. 21: 185-222.

REININK, G.J.
1972   "Das Problem des Ursprungs des Testamentes
        Adams." *Orientalia Christiana Analecta*. 197: 387-99.

1983   "Der Verfassername 'Modios' der syrischen
        Schatzhöhle und die Apokalypse des Pseudo-
        Methodius." *Oriens Christianus*. 67: 46-64.

RENAN, E.
1853   "Fragments du livre gnostique intitulé Apocalypse
        d'Adam, ou Pénitence d'Adam ou Testament
        d'Adam." *Journal Asiatique*. 5 (2): 427-71.

RI, SU-MIN
1987   *La Caverne des Trésors. Les deux recensions*.
        Corpus Scriptorum Christianorum Orientalium 486-
        487, Scriptores Syriaci 207-208. Louvain, Peeters.

RIESSLER, P.
1928   *Altjüdisches Schrifttum ausserhalb der Bibel.*
Heidelberg, Kerle.

ROBINSON, S.E.
1982   *The Testament of Adam: An Examination of the Syriac and Greek Traditions.* Society of Biblical Literature Dissertation Series 52. vol. 52. Chico CA, Scholars Press.

1983   "Testament of Adam." *The Old Testament Pseudepigrapha.* ed. J.H. Charlesworth. Garden City, Doubleday, 1: 989-995.

1985   "The Testament of Adam and the Angelic Liturgy." *Revue d Qumran.* 12: 105-110.

RUSSELL, J.R.
1987   *Yovhannēs T'lkuranc'i and the Mediaeval Armenian Lyric Tradition.* University of Pennsylvania Armenian Texts and Studies 7. ed. M. E. Stone. Atlanta, Scholars Press.

SCHÄFER, P.
1977   "Adam II. Im Frühjudentum." *Theologische Realenzyklopädie.* Berlin, de Gruyter, 1: 424-427.

1986   "Adam in jüdischen Überlieferung." *Vom alten zum neuen Adam: Urzeitmythos und Heilsgeschichte.* ed. W. Strolz. Freiburg, Basel and Vienna, Herder, 69-93.

SCHNEEMELCHER, W AND HENNECKE, E.
1973-1975 *New Testament Apocrypha* trans. by R. McL. Wilson. London: SCM.

SCHÖNFELDER, J.M.
1866   *Salomonis episc. bassorensis liber Apis.* Bamberg.

SCHULTZ, D. R.
1978 "The Origin of Sin in Irenaeus and Jewish Pseudepigraphical Literature." *Vigiliae Christianae.* 32: 161-190.

SCHÜRER, E.
1893 Review of Jagič *Theologische Literatur-Zeitung.* (16): 398-99.

1909 *Geschichte des jüdischen Volkes im Zeitalter Jesu Christi.* 4 ed. 3 vols. Leipzig, Hinrichs.

1973, 1979, 1986 *The History of the Jewish People in the Age of Jesus Christ.* ed. G. Vermes and F. Millar. Edinburgh, T. & T.Clark.

SEYMOUR, ST.J.D.
1922 "The Book of Adam and Eve in Ireland." *Proceedings of the Royal Irish Academy.* 36 C: 121-133.

SHARPE, J.L.
1969 *Prolegomena to the Establishment of the Critical Text of the Greek Apocalypse of Moses.* Ph.D dissertation. Duke University.

1973 "The Second Adam in the Apocalypse of Moses." *Catholic Biblical Quarterly.* 35: 35-46.

SIMON, J.
1941 "Notes bibliographiques sur les textes de la "Chrestomathia Aethiopica" de A. Dillmann." *Orientalia.* 10: 285-311.

SIMON, M.
1970 "Adam et la rédemption dans la perspective de l'église ancienne." *Types of Redemption.* ed. R. J. Z. Werblowsky and C. J. Bleeker. Leiden, Brill, 62-71.

SOISALON-SOININEN, I.
1965 *Die Infinitive in der Septuaginta.* Helsinki, Finnish Academy.

SPARKS, H.F.D.
1984   *The Apocryphal Old Testament.* Oxford, Clarendon Press.

SQUIRE, A. K.
1980   "Adam's Song in a Commentary of Hilary of Poitiers." *Studia Patristica,* 17.1. ed. E. Livingstone. 338-342.

STEGMÜLLER, F.
1950   *Repertorium Biblicum Medii Aevi.* No. 74, 26-27, 28. Madrid, Instituto Francisco Suárez.

STICHEL, R.
1971   *Die Namen Noes, seines Bruders und seiner Frau.* Göttingen, Vandenhoeck und Ruprecht.

1989   "Die Verführung der Stammeltern durch Satanael nach der Kurzfassung der slavischen Baruch-Apokalypse." *Kulturelle Traditionen in Bulgarian.* ed. R. Lauer and P. Schreiner. Vandenhoeck und Ruprecht, Göttingen, 116-128.

STOKES, W.
1862   *Three Irish Glossaries.* London. (*non vidi*).

1884   "Man Octipartite. From the Middle Irish." *Academy.* 26: 236. (*non vidi*).

STONE, M.E.
1966   "The Death of Adam: An Armenian Adam Book." *Harvard Theological Review.* 59: 283-291.

1976   "Armenian Canon Lists III - The Lists of Mechitar of Ayrivank'." *Harvard Theological Review.* 69: 289-300.

1981a   *The Penitence of Adam.* Corpus Scriptorum Christianorum Orientalium 429-30; Scriptores Armeniaci 13-14. ed. R. Draguet. Leuven, Peeters.

1981b   "Report on Seth Traditions in the Armenian Adam Books." *The Rediscovery of Gnosticism.* ed. B. Layton. Leiden, Brill, 2: 460-471.

1981c   *Signs of the Judgment, Onomastica Sacra and The Generations from Adam.* University of Pennsylvania Armenian Texts and Studies 3. ed. M. E. Stone. Chico CA, Scholars Press.

1982   *Armenian Apocrypha Relating to Patriarchs and Prophets.* Jerusalem, Israel Academy of Sciences.

1984   "The History of the Forefathers, Adam and His Sons and Grandsons." *Journal of the Society of Armenian Studies.* 1: 79-91.

1990   Review of D.A. Bertrand, *La Vie grecque d'Adam et d'Eve* (1987). *Critical Review of Books in Religion.* 2:333-336.

under preparation   *Armenian Apocrypha: Relating to the Protoplasts.* Jerusalem, Israel Academy of Sciences and Humanities.

SUIDAS

1971   "'Αδάμ" *Suidae Lexicon.* ed. A. Adler. Stuttgart, Teubner, 1: 43-46.

TARCHNISHVILI, M.

1955   *Geschichte der kirchlichen georgischen Literatur.* Studi e Testi 185. Rome, Vatican.

THOMSON, S. H.

1933   "A Fifth Recension of the Latin 'Vita Ade et Eve'." *Studi Medievali.* NS 6: 271-278.

TICHONRAVOV, N.S.

1863   Памятники отреченной русской литературы (*Monuments of Russian Apocryphal Literature*). St. Petersburg.

TISCHENDORF, C. VON
    1866   *Apocalypses Apocryphae Mosis, Esdrae, Pauli, Iohanni...* Leipzig, Mendelssohn; rerp. Hildersheim, Olms, 1966.

TORREY, C.C.
    1945   *The Apocryphal Literature.* New Haven, Yale University Press.

TRISTRAM, H.L.C.
    1975   "Der "homo octipartitus" in der irischen und altenglischen Literatur." *Zeitschrift für Celtische Philologie.* 34: 119-153.

TROJE, L.
    1916   "AΔAM und ZΩH: Eine szene der altchristlichen Kunst in ihrem religionsgeschichtliche Zusammengange." *Sitzungsberichte der Heidleberger Akademie der Wissenschaften Philos.-hist Kl.* Abh. 17.

TRUMPP, E.
    1881   "Der Kampf Adams, oder Das christliche Adambuch des Morgenlandes, Äthiopischer Text, verglichen mit dem arabischen Originaltext." *Abhandlungen der philosophisch-philologischen Classe der königlichen Bayerischen Akademie der Wissenschaften, philos.-philol. Classe.* 15 (3): 1-172.

    1882   "Das Hexaëmeron des Pseudo-Epiphanius. äthiopischer Text verglichen mit dem arabischen Originaltext und deutscher Übersetzung." *Abhandlungen der philosophisch-philologischen Classe der königlichen Bayerischen Akademie der Wissenschaften, philos.-philol. Classe.* vol. 16 (2).

TURDEANU, É.
    1981   *Apocryphes slaves et roumains de l'Ancien Testament.* Studia in Veteris Testamenti Pseudepigrapha, 5. Leiden, Brill.

TURNER, N.
1976   "Style." *A Grammar of New Testament Greek,* ed. J.
            H. Moulton. Vol. 4. Edinburgh, T. and T. Clark.

TZAFERIS, V.
1987   *The Monastery of the Holy Cross in Jerusalem.*
            Jerusalem, Tzaferis.

VASSILIEV, A.
1893   *Anecdota Graeco-Byzantina.* Moscow, Imperial
            University.

VAUGHAN, M.F.
1983   "The Prophets of the Anglo-Norman 'Adam'."
            Traditio. 39: 81-114.

VOGL, A.
1979   "Adam - Messias in der Schatzhöhle." *Ostkirchliche
            Studien.* 28: 183-185.

WALKER, A.
1986   "Revelation of Moses." *The Ante-Nicene Fathers.*
            Grand Rapids MI, Eerdmans, reprint of 1870 edition.
            8: 565-570.

WEISS, H.D.
1989   "A Schema of 'The Rond' in Philo and Lucan."
            Studia Philonica Annual. 1: 43-57.

WELLS, L.S.A.
1913   "The Books of Adam and Eve." *The Apocrypha and
            Pseudepigrapha of the Old Testament.* ed. R. H.
            Charles. Oxford, Oxford University Press, 2: 123-54.

WHITTAKER, M.
1984   "The Life of Adam and Eve." *The Apocryphal Old
            Testament.* ed. H. F. D. Sparks. Oxford, Clarendon
            Press, 141-167.

WRIGHT, W.
1865   *Contributions to the Apocryphal Literature of the
            N.T.* London, Williams and Northgate.

YOVSĒP'IANC', S.

1898   *Անկանոն Գիրք Հին Կտակարանաց (Uncanonical Books of the Old Testament).* Venice, Mechitarist Press.

ZEEGERS-VANDER VORST, N.

1981   "Satan, Eve et le serpent chez Théophile d'Antioche." *Vigiliae Christianae.* 35: 152-169.

ZIEGLER, J. (ED.)

1975   *Eusebius' Werke,* vol. 9. Berlin, Akademie Verlag.

INDEX